Comfy Shoes and Keychains

Comfy Shoes and Keychains

Tips for Women in Leadership

Carrie Hruby

ROWMAN & LITTLEFIELD
Lanham • Boulder • New York • London

Published by Rowman & Littlefield
An imprint of The Rowman & Littlefield Publishing Group, Inc.
4501 Forbes Boulevard, Suite 200, Lanham, Maryland 20706
www.rowman.com

86-90 Paul Street, London EC2A 4NE, United Kingdom

British Library Cataloguing in Publication Information Available

Library of Congress Cataloging-in-Publication Data

Names: Hruby, Carrie, 1947– author.
Title: Comfy shoes and keychains : tips for women in leadership / Carrie Hruby.
Description: Lanham : Rowman & Littlefield, [2024] | Includes bibliographical
   references. | Summary: "In Comfy Shoes and Keychains, Hruby uses the power
   of storytelling to provide tips and insightful lessons on confidence, self-care,
   communication, engagement, burnout and more. Each chapter tells the story of a
   woman in leadership who faces adversity and learns to overcome. The book offers
   insight to fears and struggles that are relatable to all leaders. The stories are real and
   heartfelt and provide valuable tips for resilience and success. From the guilt of a
   working mom to the need to fight for equity, Hruby inspires leaders while coaching
   them through each narrative. Hruby inspires women to be successful leaders while
   empowering them to write their own story. She challenges women to push back
   against gender bias and inspires them to shatter glass ceilings of opportunity"—
   Provided by publisher.
Identifiers: LCCN 2023030314 (print) | LCCN 2023030315 (ebook) | ISBN
   9781475872859 (cloth) | ISBN 9781475872866 (paperback) | ISBN
   9781475872873 (epub)
Subjects: LCSH: Leadership in women. | Women executives. | Resilience (Personality
   trait) in women. | Glass ceiling (Employment discrimination) | Communication in
   management.
Classification: LCC HD6054.3 .H73 2024 (print) | LCC HD6054.3 (ebook) | DDC
   658.4/09082—dc23/eng/20231002
LC record available at https://lccn.loc.gov/2023030314
LC ebook record available at https://lccn.loc.gov/2023030315

To Tammijean Kuhn—the greatest and most courageous leader of us all. May we find your love, joy, and faith in our hearts every day. And may we always remember your favorite lesson, "In a world where you can be anything, be kind."

Contents

Foreword

The topic of women in leadership has been around for many years, yet here we are in 2023 and still in desperate need of important work in this area. Whether you are a wife, mom, daughter, sister, aunt, or friend or you're a man reading this to learn more about women, we all need books that highlight women and their successes and challenges.

When Dr. Carrie Hruby told me she was writing a book surrounding the topic of women leaders, I was beyond excited because I knew it would be a rational, practical, and strategic approach to this work while also highlighting the importance and value of creating effective relationships. And she's delivered all of that in what I hope is the first of many books for her.

Hruby's book takes us on a journey of self-exploration into the topic of women in leadership, but more importantly, this book makes us reflect on our own leadership and personal experiences and the stories that result from them. It makes us think about our abilities to build effective relationships in our lives and organizations and reflect on how we express our appreciation for others around us. This book helps us through leadership tips and guidance and gives us practical and tangible ways that we can be better for ourselves and those we serve.

In each chapter, we hear from a woman who likely struggles with the same challenges that we do on a daily basis. From Susan to Erica to Kendra, we see ourselves in their stories. Hruby subtly, yet brilliantly, sets the stage for us to learn from others, yet she also challenges us to strive to make ourselves better. Key points of confidence, ego, empathy, arrogance, and caring are highlighted in ways that allow us to be honest with ourselves and strive to be better in our organizations. The stories are real and heartfelt, and Hruby's leadership tips are exactly what we all need to hear.

One of the most powerful pieces of Hruby's work is the concept of the keychain. In this particular section, she highlights the strong sense of responsibility that women have in their leadership roles and gives us ways to detach from the role but still be who we need to be as people. Carrie actually gave me a keychain several years ago, and I still have it with the solid reminders of the "why" behind it. To see her write about this concept for the world to see is inspiring, engaging, and empowering for all women leaders, who will likely go buy themselves or a colleague a keychain after reading her work.

From mom guilt to the mountaintop moment to being a champion for equity, Hruby covers it all in this powerful yet relatable book. While we reflect about our own leadership and experiences, we leave feeling a sense of understanding, and we leave feeling seen as women. And then, Hruby gives us the final push we need to reflect on what's next for ourselves and our own journeys and encourages us to go out and tell our own stories.

And finally, while many of us dread putting on those five-inch heels, Hruby allows us to wear our comfy shoes and feel like the confident, determined, and successful women that we are. Enjoy this inspiring book, encourage others to read it, and go out and share your story.

—Dr. Courtney Orzel
Author of *Unsupervised Leadership*; co-host of *Unsupervised Leadership* podcast series; and associate director of professional development, Illinois Association of School Administrators

Preface

Leadership is synonymous with stress. By design, the leader of an organization is the one individual who faces the most challenging decisions and the most pressure. Leaders are not only evaluated but often publicly judged based on their ability to handle stressful situations. A leader who is able to remain poised and collected during a heated crisis or debate is viewed as trustworthy and competent. Conversely, a leader who struggles to maintain composure and overreacts with anger or emotion risks losing credibility indefinitely. But what is the best way to handle stress, and is it a skill that can be taught?

I have vivid childhood memories of my family driving through a snowstorm with near whiteout conditions. I recall sitting in the back seat, watching and listening to my parents navigate the emotionally charged and stressful circumstances. I remember closing my eyes and trying to sleep until it was all over and we were safely home. In hindsight, I recognize now that my tool for dealing with the stress of the storm and hazardous ride was to tune out. The situation felt out of my control. The ability to close my eyes and deafen the fears was a critical tool for me because I had no control over the environment as a child. The only option I had was to check out mentally and emotionally.

Now, as a middle-aged adult, my solutions to handling stress are not as simple or singular. As the mom, I am responsible for navigating the car safely in the snowstorm or at the very least, helping my husband navigate the stressful situation as his copilot. I no longer have the option to close my eyes and wait for someone else to work it out. I cannot abdicate the responsibility of safety to someone else and tune out the stress as I could in childhood.

Similarly, in leadership roles, we do not have the option to close our eyes and hope someone else will find an answer or take over the situation. It is our crisis or stressful situation to navigate. The pressure is on us, and the pressure is one we often take personally and internalize. How do we deal with it? How do we proceed calmly and with poise? Every step must be intentional and strategic.

As leaders, being strategic and intentional requires us also to see ourselves as learners. It is our responsibility to be curators of our own professional development and growth. Leaders must acquire, assemble, and care for a collection of skills and knowledge. We must also ensure learning permeates every aspect of the organization, which means staff will also need to be provided a safe space to be vulnerable and candid about what they do not know. This book serves as a celebration of the unique skills women bring to leadership and a guide to improving skills through the stories of women who lead.

Leadership is challenging. Women in leadership battle preconceived misconceptions of our ability to be confident, decisive, and firm while remaining empathetic and flexible. Some people cast judgment about whether a female leader can be tough enough to handle stressful situations without coming across as cold and uncaring. Others judge whether a female leader can juggle home and work while raising a family in a demanding professional position. I've received these judgments personally, even openly and overtly.

After eight years of successful service as the assistant superintendent in a large school district, I was encouraged to apply for the vacancy of the superintendent. Honored to apply, I knew the seven board members were familiar with my successful experience in the district. They had a front-row seat to the success I had in the role of assistant superintendent. On the morning of my interview for the promotion, I confidently walked into the room to see all seven board members seated around a table. Our interactions were more formal than usual because the group was cautious to ensure they followed the interview protocols equally for all candidates. The interview started very well, and I felt comfortable being myself because they knew me well already. They knew the leadership I had provided the district for almost a decade. I had proven my ability to lead the organization as its second in command and first in command when the superintendent was away from his office.

While that interview was many years ago, I can still vividly remember one specific point at the end of the interview when the board president asked if any of his fellow board members had additional questions to ask before they wrapped up the hour-long interview. After a brief pause, one male board member, who at the time had a son and a daughter in the district, uttered, "I'm not sure how to ask this." He paused briefly, then continued confidently, "What about . . . I would like to ask her . . . what about the gender question?"

I froze. I wasn't sure I heard him correctly. I was caught off guard by his off-the-cuff stream-of-consciousness innuendo. Until that moment, it had never occurred to me that they might see me differently than other candidates because I was a female leader. I was the first female superintendent candidate they had ever interviewed. Unbeknownst to me, I walked into the room with barriers my competition did not have solely because I was female.

This board member judged whether or not I was able to handle the pressures of the top position solely because of my gender. He expected me to explain how my gender would influence my ability to lead. Not only would I be their first female superintendent, but I would also be the youngest superintendent in the district's history. However, it was not my age or years of experience he doubted. It was not my age or maturity he audibly questioned. It was my gender.

Fortunately, the board member sitting next to him had professional experience in human resources and quickly cut off his covert sexism, snapping, "You can't ask her that." He turned toward her and began to debate with her, replying, "Why not?" (This was the year 2012, by the way!) She stopped him again and firmly declared, "You cannot ask her that question." Upon witnessing his gender bias, the rest of the group displayed disapproval in their facial expressions and body language. They quickly redirected my attention to their interview wrap-up and brushed off his attempt to put me on the spot.

In my role as the assistant superintendent, this individual had never questioned my leadership. Rather than empowering a young female leader who had already proven herself successful, he was more interested in questioning my place at the table. He was focused on asking me to justify how I could lead a dynamic organization with a multimillion-dollar budget and five hundred employees . . . as a woman.

Had I not felt certain I was a strong candidate for the position, the moment would have significantly shaken my self-confidence. And had I not already been acquainted with this group of board members, my nerves would have shaken me when he unfairly implied my gender would somehow influence my success as the top leader. I would have doubted my place at the table. This male board member expected me to justify what he saw as my shortcoming and disadvantage . . . I was a female leader.

My story is not uncommon for women in leadership. Women face subtle and covert gender bias and obstacles to advancement regularly. I've spoken with many women in executive leadership positions who report similar experiences. They have been asked specific questions such as how they will handle motherhood in leadership. Women are frequently judged based on physical attributes, such as being too attractive/not attractive enough, too short/too tall, too feminine/not feminine enough. Their physical attributes are used to predetermine whether they will be "tough enough" to handle the adversity and challenges of leadership or whether they will be respected. Women have been expected to address such biased presumptions as if they are deficiencies that require explanations.

Nearly every female executive leader has a similar story of gender bias. Even the most confident female leaders face judgments they must overcome.

They deserve to be lauded, supported, and celebrated for their courage and persistence. It takes strength to speak out against bias or succeed despite it.

I received an offer for the position, and it was unanimously supported by all of the seven board members. While I felt honored to receive and accept the offer, the memory of the interview remains vivid because it concluded with his hurtful and demeaning probe. Now, however, it is a memory of which I am proud. I am proud of the female leader in that room, a younger version of myself, because she didn't waiver or doubt herself. She didn't let his misogynist comment dissuade the first steps of her successful career.

Rebuilding myself from the experience required time and space, as well as a boost of confidence and self-care. But it is not enough to simply shrug off the board member's doubt when he asked me his "gender question." He was misguided and sadly mistaken about the power of a female leader and used his position of authority to communicate it. These experiences are part of my story and help empower me as a leader. They inspire me to support women in leadership who likely face similar gender bias. I hope the following stories of female leaders, whose names have been changed, will also empower you on your leadership journey.

Author's Note

Carrie dedicates this book in memory of her dear friend, who also served as an elementary principal in Carrie's former school district. Tammi was taken too soon after a courageous battle with cancer but forever remains in Carrie's heart and the hearts of those she loved and led. Following is a screenshot of a text exchange between Tammi and Carrie. The handwritten note was one Carrie handed Tammi as she escorted her into an interview room for Tammi's first administrative leadership position. She wanted Tammi to feel confident in that moment so the interview team could see what Carrie already knew— that Tammi was an incredibly talented leader. Tammi landed the job that day and went on to become a leader who made the lives of those around her better each and every day. During Tammi's battle with cancer, she sent Carrie a picture of that note she had saved for many years.

In memory of Tammi, tell those you love that you are proud of them and you believe in them! Then tell them again!

We will see you again, TK. Until then, we will try to make you proud.

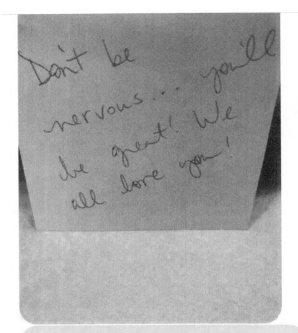

Came across this today. You handed me this as I waited for my GES AP interview. I've kept it and each time I come across it, it makes me feel loved. Love you!

Aw!!! That made my day! We loved you then and love you even more today! I've always believed you were a superstar, and you always will be one!
Love you!

Introduction

We all have a story to tell. Storytelling is one of the most authentic and practical tools for learning. This book is built around examples and stories of women in leadership, and the fears they report as part of their experiences. Each chapter is structured to illustrate the ways a leader can face and release her own fears while she finds her confidence through poise and empathy.

Apprehension and lack of confidence can hold women back in their pursuit of leadership. Fear is an emotion that stimulates a flight, fight, or freeze response as the body's ability to self-protect. From a young age, we have been conditioned to believe fear is something to avoid, a sign of weakness successful individuals don't experience.[1] We, therefore, ignore or push away fears, pretending they don't exist. Even if we ignore them, our fears stop us from attempting something new or reaching for a goal.[2] This book doesn't ignore or silence fears; rather, it amplifies and addresses them. Each chapter begins by confronting a fear, working through it with the narrative of a peer, and then using her story to spark lessons in leadership.

Rather than trying to drown out the noise of fear, a leader should learn to recognize and embrace her fear. In doing so, it is helpful to ask, "What is the worst that could happen?" By articulating and naming the worst outcome and then recognizing it isn't likely to happen, you are able to persist in spite of the fear. The fear is, therefore, not allowed to consume nor control.

For example, perhaps you could inaccurately predict annual revenues and skew the organization's budget projections. The error would be embarrassing and would need to be fixed. But the chances of being fired are very unlikely because in this scenario, it would not always be possible to accurately predict the state's appropriation of funds. Naming the worst that could happen, a termination, and then also recognizing that it is not likely to occur decreases the significance of the fear. Taking it a step further, remind yourself that even if that worst outcome would occur, there would be other job opportunities in organizations that could be more supportive and understanding.

Labeling a fear keeps it from being inflated or bigger than it actually is. Sharing it allows other women to see their own fears are not uncommon. I've interviewed women in leadership positions about their fears. Their fears mirror the commonly articulated fears women face of failing, being judged, and not being liked.[3] In my conversations with them about leadership, they label some of their fears as:

"Not being liked, in a very public role,"

"Not being able to endure the stress and pressure of the leadership position,"

"Not being respected,"

"Appearing weak or inadequate,"

"Not being accepted by male colleagues or bosses,"

"Failing as a working mother with not enough time in a day,"

"Not knowing enough or being as accomplished as my peers,"

"Not being able to lead the organization through conflict,"

"Being misunderstood,"

"Losing sight of my 'why,' the legacy I want to leave," and

"Having the courage to do what is right, even when it means doing what is hard."

This list is not surprising. As women, we often underestimate ourselves.[4] Female leaders allow these fears to become weaknesses that hold us back from success. If we allow them to, fears or doubt can serve as a weight to slow or pull a leader down. We ruminate about the thoughts of what might happen if we fail. This type of uncertainty and self-doubt is a waste of energy. It serves as a distraction from the work.

Fears distract or hold us back from achievements. The fear of failure itself is strong and pervasive for a female leader and can stand in the way of her ambition and effectiveness. We hesitate to pursue lofty achievements when we ruminate on possible failures. But when taken head-on and embraced, self-doubts merely signal respect for the leadership position and a strong desire to be successful. Quite literally, fears are nothing of which to be afraid.

This book aims to dig further into common fears for women in leadership and offers tips for resilience and success. To better understand the way leaders overcome adversity, it is helpful to apply the Resilience Theoretical Framework. Resilience theory provides insight for leaders who wish to survive, recover, or thrive after facing adversity, hardship, stress, or challenge.[5]

Resilience theory addresses the ability to overcome adversity or an adverse situation by not only surviving but thriving through adversity. Leaders face adversity and distress in decisions they make; situations through which they lead; and challenges from employees, colleagues, and supervisors. Resilience theory points to thriving as the ability to come out on the other side stronger, more optimistic, more determined, and more powerful than before.[6] Taking into consideration the pressures and stress of leadership positions, resilience theory is a critical component of leadership endurance. A leader must be courageous enough to tackle her own self-doubt. This book provides illustrations of resilience from which leaders can learn.

There must be a balance between tackling fears with confidence in a leadership role and approaching the position with an ego and lack of empathy. The stories of female leaders told in this book also explore the effect humility and empathy have on success in leadership. Women in leadership commonly believe they need to portray an assertive, bold style. That leadership style can be mistaken for a strong ego, which can actually be detrimental to building culture and climate and addressing workplace wellness.

Leadership requires empathy, confidence, optimism, and competence. The capacity for leadership is built by supportive partnerships with peers and supervisors, collaboration opportunities with trusted colleagues, the ability to partner with colleagues, time for reflection and collaboration, and reduction in social isolation.[7] A leader with a strong ego can deteriorate an organization because ego is centered on self, unlike empathy which is focused on the needs of others. Ego is what makes us compare ourselves to others' materials or achievements.[8] Such comparisons are destructive. Empathy not only protects the leader's emotional well-being but also those she leads.

Fortunately, empathy and resilience are skills that can be taught and improved. The stories told in this book offer lessons in resilience because each female leader learned to thrive in the face of adversity or challenges. Their stories are offered as a support to other leaders who might be struggling with similar challenges.

Partially based on these challenges for women in leadership, it is commonly understood that there are fewer women in executive leadership roles than men. But the question of how to best support and encourage women in leadership should not be limited to underrepresentation. Initiatives for women in leadership should not only be focused on increasing the number of women in executive positions. They should also focus on developing and supporting women in leadership.[9] This book uses the power of storytelling to provide you with tips for care and confidence so you too may embrace the influential female leader you already are!

Chapter 1

Comfy Shoes and Care for the Organization

Women in leadership say they fear "Not being liked in a very public role."

Women in leadership often report a desire to be liked, while their male counterparts say they want to be respected. Both want to be seen as strong leaders, but women tend to want to please others or make them happy.

Being a good leader can be characterized by a specific set of skills while being a great leader is also defined by vulnerability, empathy, and engagement. An engaged leader is the one in the room wearing comfy shoes. She wears comfy shoes to intentionally remove obstacles from her path toward authentically engaging with the team. She is willing to get out of her desk chair; move throughout the organization; and approach individuals in personal, face-to-face interactions. She wants to laugh with, smile with, and enjoy moments with her staff and colleagues.

MIA'S LEADERSHIP STORY

Mia was a leader who exuded confidence and had a strong sense of ethics. She had the desire to do what was best for the organization. She exemplified what author Jim Collins refers to as a Level 5 leader because she carried a strong will and was ambitious first and foremost for her organization rather than for a self-serving purpose or stepping stone to other opportunities.[1]

When Mia decided to become an administrator, she promised she would never treat a position as a stepping stone. She only wanted to serve in leadership roles in which she could be a Level 5 leader,[2] and even if she aspired to move ahead in her career, her core value system told her she would be steadfast in her aspirations for the organization, rather than herself as an individual.

Although she was the top official in her role as superintendent of schools, Mia was the type of leader who never let herself think "That's not my job." Mia held a strong sense of loyalty to the organization and saw no task as a task beneath her position. She would walk into a school building for a meeting and pick up trash on her way in. Or she would pull weeds as she noticed them from the sidewalk.

While the management of trash and weeds was not in her job description, she never hesitated because she cared for her schools and the individuals inside them. She simply thought she was on her way into the school anyway; it wouldn't hurt to spend a few seconds improving the grounds while she strolled to the door. Mia's aspirations for the school district outweighed any type of ego.

Mia was a self-proclaimed shoe lover. She loved to dress up an outfit with a great pair of heels. Shoes and jewelry were her jam. She admittedly was addicted to shopping for accessories. Her closet overflowed with shoes in every color. From peep-toe to patent leather, she had a perfect match for every outfit. All of her dress pants were hemmed to a length that required her to wear pumps with them, and she loved to finish an outfit with a great pair of fashionable shoes.

As she rose in her leadership role over two decades, Mia's feet started to hurt more at the end of the day. She noticed after walking all day in her favorite pumps, she would quickly kick them off at the steps of her garage before she went into her house. On the weekends, she preferred to wear tennis shoes or flip-flops because her feet needed a break.

Mia noticed she subconsciously chose to sit idly in her office on the days she wore shoes that rubbed her heels. She became more disengaged with the staff in her schools, and her job energy and satisfaction waned. One day a rooftop unit in one of her schools needed significant repairs. While Mia was no subject matter expert in the area of HVAC, her director of facilities felt she needed to see what was happening before approving the sizable expenditure for the repairs. Mia agreed, and the director escorted her to the flat, rubber-barrier roof.

Before they stepped out the rooftop door, Mia froze, realizing she could never walk on the rubber lining with her heels. She kicked them off at the door, and even though her feet were covered in black when they were finished, she was able to see the extent of the damage he wanted to show her.

After that, Mia chose to keep a comfortable pair of shoes in her car. She noticed her comfy shoes did not simply come in handy during her visits to a rooftop, which were few and far between. Her new comfortable shoes allowed unrestricted movement throughout the organization. Her subconscious deterrent for walking hours at a time through buildings was thwarted when she gave herself an alternative.

Mia's staff did not see her as any less professional than when she would don a fancy pair of shoes. In fact, she was held in higher regard because she was visible and active. She realized she could have asked her director to send a picture of the HVAC unit, but seeing it in person and talking through the next steps with him face-to-face enabled Mia to build a trusting relationship and be actively engaged in the organization.

While comfortable shoes meet a practical need and help avoid blisters, a symbol of social comfort in walking around is perhaps of greater importance in Mia's lessons. A leader who is comfortable engaging directly with colleagues and staff is a leader who models her value of team and her transparency in her role. Foot blisters bring physical pain, but the sores and scars left from battles of making unpopular decisions can be more challenging to heal. A leader who actively creates and cultivates relationships is a leader who can weather those challenges.

There were days Mia would spend hours crunching financial data, sorting through board politics, or researching applicable laws for an employee discipline issue. When overwhelmed with the position's stress, she would often take a trip to one of the schools. She said it helped her recharge and remember the most important pieces of her job were those most impactful to students' lives. Mia's face-to-face interactions with students and staff reignited her passion on challenging days.

LEARNING FROM MIA'S LEADERSHIP STORY

Relationship building requires small steps, taken daily, to model respect and appreciation for others. Uncomfortable shoes represent a roadblock to face-to-face engagement. When sporting a trendy, toe-pinching pair of heels rubbing the side of the foot into blisters, it is much easier to sit passively behind a desk and manage via email or phone calls. When a leader wears uncomfortable shoes, the path of least resistance is to disengage, sit back quietly, and react with little motivation.

Conversely, a comfy pair of flat, well-fitting, cushioned shoes belongs to the leader who wants to break down barriers to visiting team members and interacting in a personable way. She is a leader who is on the go and engaging. She is a proactive leader with a laser-focused vision for the organization and her role within it.

More often than not, a comfortable shoe is the perfect fit for a high-profile, visible leader who puts care for the organization before her own agenda. She is willing to take steps to build trust and loyalty physically. Not only does a comfy-shoe-wearing, engaged leader walk around, but she also finds ways to engage with staff in a personal way. The imagery of comfy shoes represents a desire to connect to individuals and build relationships with them.

While there are many occasions for a pair of fancy shoes, when a leader puts on a pair of comfy shoes she is ready to be on the go, personalizing active leadership. She looks employees in the eye and actively listens to their input and their concerns. She makes attempts to know them personally, at least at a tertiary level, and uses their names to address them. It matters not to her what title they hold: custodian, principal, teacher, bus driver, board member. The success of the organization depends on each of them. Not one can do the work of all. They are each essential in their own way. As a leader, she knows all deserve her attention and respect.

Her ability to build relationships begins with conversations and face-to-face, eye-to-eye interactions. She genuinely listens and cares. She knows even a brief greeting and short interchange can positively affect someone's day. A conversation with genuine eye contact and addressing an employee by name sends a message she is considerate and values the employee.

"Remember that a person's name is to that person the sweetest and most important sound in any language."[3] When a person in a position of influence or power addresses an individual using eye contact and addressing by name, the feeling received is one of being worthy, accepted, and appreciated.

A leader must be present with an employee to look the individual in the eye and hear what is being shared. This requires active listening. Active listening is actually a sign of strength, as it requires restraint. It shows an employee their leader is not too busy to care. When a leader focuses on being reflective and thoughtful as she listens, she is able to be in the moment without distraction. Often an employee will initiate a conversation with a leader by saying, "I know you're busy, but . . ." This is a cue the employee does not feel like a priority. The leader should seize the opportunity to shift the assumption by putting down a phone or other work and replying, "I am not too busy for you; please share your thoughts with me."

Staff also need to know they are appreciated. No one ever said, "My boss appreciates me too much." Positive workplace environments are those in which employees feel they matter at work. There is a culture of gratitude and recognition, which are connected to the vision of the organization.[4]

While public praise is most often well received, there is a risk to public recognition of individuals. If a leader recognizes one employee with an honor that only she receives, there is a chance that others will feel they are not worthy or will become frustrated, rather than motivated, to achieve the same. And the individual who receives the formal recognition then may feel ostracized by peers because she was singled out. In those situations, notecards can be a more positive way to recognize because they are personal and the individual can keep them forever.

Handwritten notes of praise and recognition can build strong relationships. Order personalized notecards with your organization's logo. The physical act of handwriting notes to staff can become a positive, mindful ritual for a leader. Taking a quiet moment to handwrite celebrations and compliments can also be calming for the leader who is writing the note. Similar to the cathartic energy from journaling, the practice of writing positive notes of gratitude brings good energy to the leader, as well as her staff members who receive the positive notes.

Messages written to staff should be genuine and specific, rather than a simple thank-you note for being present or completing an expected job task. A note of appreciation should highlight a specific accomplishment or skill set/ talent. However, telling or even showing staff you value them is not enough. A leader must also be transparent at the same time. Value and transparency must go hand in hand.

Value minus transparency feels fake or forged. Staff need to trust that the leadership is transparent in how the organization is being led. If a leader says she values staff but then behaves in a manner that is not transparent, her staff do not believe she respects them. The words feel fake or forged. Staff see it as lip service even if she displays tokens of appreciation. If she is not open and honest about decisions or plans, staff do not believe her when she says she values them.

Transparency without value exposes the leader as an uncaring individual. If a leader acts transparently and explains her thoughts and plans but does not genuinely respect and care about staff, she comes across as cold-hearted and insincere. Both value and transparency must be part of the culture of the organization.

VALUE

A leader's responsibility is to fluently articulate and model her value of staff and appreciation of their skills and effort. It is not enough to assume staff members know they are appreciated or respected. Appreciation and gratitude should be communicated. The leader should find ways to celebrate achievements, offer a shout-out for hard work, or simply thank staff for their commitment with a handwritten note.

An effective way to express gratitude is through handwritten notes mailed to staff, colleagues, or students. There are many free design software programs to create inexpensive, personalized notecards with the organization's logo and a leader's name and title.

At the beginning of every week, place five notecards on your desk as a reminder to send appreciation or shout-outs to students or staff. Simply placing five notecards on the edge of the desk can be an intentional way to ensure they are sent. The blank notes on the edge of a desk serve as a regular reminder throughout the week to prioritize and complete this meaningful task. It takes only a few minutes per note but can leave a lasting impression on those who receive a personalized message.

While notes of appreciation and treats or trinkets are delightful, genuinely expressing gratitude and respect must extend beyond letters written or treats purchased by a leader. An intentional appreciation plan consists of several layers, including handwritten notes, email messages, treats, verbal praise, awards, public recognition, opportunities for growth, and of course, compensation. Each is used by a leader who cares for and values employees.

It also goes without saying that employees feel valued by their compensation and benefits, but leaders of school systems may not have control over those specifics. A negotiated contract outlines compensation details for multiple years, and a board most likely makes compensation decisions. However, there are plenty of ways a leader helps employees feel valued besides compensation.

When a leader genuinely values staff and cares for the organization, she also asks staff for their input. She wants to have a pulse on their perspective. She knows it is her responsibility to acknowledge their feedback, then put it to use. For example, if staff members are asked to complete a survey and offer feedback, the leader must report back the aggregated survey results. The employees will then be able to hear their own voices and see the information put to use. In this way, she shows them they are being listened to and their input is essential.

The way a leader shows she values staff is also reflected in how she coaches and redirects them. Although there will always be some employees who do not meet expectations or follow procedures, leaders and managers should set the default to treating everyone well.[5] If policies or rules are written based on the poor employees, all feel punished, and the poor employees think they are one of many who act poorly because all are treated the same while trying not to blame certain staff.

Communicating in response to feedback should also be thoughtful, honest, and transparent. Messaging matters. What you say, how you say it, and the intent behind the message all matter. For example, valuing others means using the word *but* cautiously. A straightforward phrase that includes the word *but* can be dangerous. If you say, "I want your input, but . . ." or "I am sorry, but . . ." or even "I appreciate you, but . . . ," everything after the word *but* negates the first part of the statement. The word itself is a trigger and can serve as a dismissal of the message a leader tries to convey.

TRANSPARENCY

Employees will only feel truly valued if they also feel there is a reasonable level of transparency in the organization and decisions made by leadership. They want and need to know how decisions are made and what the leader prioritizes. They need to know where they fit into those decisions and priorities. Transparency builds a trusting relationship.

A leader can express and model gratitude. However, if the expression is coupled with a lack of communication while everything happening within the organization comes as a surprise, the employee will not trust the appreciation efforts. As a leader, you must communicate openly and honestly, to the extent possible. There will always be topics or issues that must remain confidential and cannot be shared with employees or publicly. However, if nothing is shared, you will appear aloof and uncaring as the leader. Employees should be told information about the health and vision of the organization. They should also be privy to details about where the organization is headed and how it will get there.

A leader's efforts to be transparent must be genuine, or employees will see right through them. Communication from leadership to staff should be clear and honest. Staff are less likely to gossip or rumor if they are provided details about the organization. Leaving staff in the dark will only provoke resistance and resentment.

Women in leadership have the ability to model open and honest leadership by the way they care for those within the organization. Leading in comfy shoes is leading in a personal way, showing appreciation for staff in face-to-face conversations. It is a symbol of the walk of leadership guided by transparency and trust.

LEADERSHIP TIPS

- Comfortable shoes are a metaphor for engaged leadership.
- Keeping a pair of comfortable shoes in the office allows a leader to be on the go.
- Comfortable shoes give rise to face-to-face engagement with staff.
- Express recognition and gratitude. No one says, "My leader thanks me too much."
- Display transparency in sharing as much information about the organization as is appropriate.

Chapter 2

Confidence

Women in leadership say they fear "Not being respected," "Appearing weak or inadequate," and "Not being accepted by male colleagues or bosses."

The role of a leader is one of pressure and high cognitive demand. It is not uncommon for leaders to battle the imposter syndrome, feeling underskilled and underprepared for the role. Too often, though, women are less confident in their abilities than their male counterparts. They assume everyone else is confident and they are alone in their fears. Addressing fears requires being confident.

Some of the most accomplished female leaders question their personal effectiveness. Even the most seasoned and experienced leaders have moments of self-doubt and fear. Many women in leadership report feeling plagued with self-doubt. Building confidence is key to success as a woman in leadership. Confidence inspires action but also reduces fear and anxiety and contributes to emotional well-being.[1]

SUSAN'S LEADERSHIP STORY

Susan serves as a second-grade teacher and has recently decided to apply for administrative positions. She searched resumes online to find a template she could use as a model for her own. The example she selected allowed her to highlight the ways in which she served as a leader in her teaching position. Susan gathered letters of recommendation from her principal and superintendent and was proud to see they believed she would be an excellent administrator. She thought to herself, "They know me well, and know the position they've served in for years. Their encouragement must mean I'm ready."

Susan was pleased to receive an opportunity to interview for an assistant principal position in a nearby high school. She had five days to prepare and was eager to show them she would be the perfect candidate. Susan spent four days picking out the perfect gray pantsuit with a red accent blouse. She planned her attire, down to the earrings and bracelet she would wear, making sure they were subtle enough to not draw too much attention to any one accessory. She was ready.

On the day of the interview, Susan walked into the room smartly dressed, feeling confident and excited. She remembered the good advice her principal Nancy gave her. Nancy helped Susan prepare for the interview by telling her she should just be herself. Quite simply, Nancy said the person who shows up for an interview must be able to show up for the job every day. She explained that while some people think they can pretend to be someone they are not, leaders must present their genuine selves to ensure a good fit in a school district and a position. Nancy went on to tell Susan if she focused on being herself, her nerves would be more controlled because when we are true to ourselves, there's no need to be nervous.

Susan sat in the waiting room before the interview and negative thoughts entered her mind. She began to doubt whether she would be able to impress the interviewers. Her thoughts raced about whether she would measure up to the other candidates. Susan took a deep breath and remembered Nancy's advice.

When she was introduced to the interview team of teachers, the principal, and the school secretary, Susan greeted them with a genuine smile, knowing it was her smile they needed to see and her as an individual they would most appreciate. Susan felt herself roll her shoulders back as she took another deep breath and sat a few inches taller. She held her hands above the table and felt natural in her conversation with the team. While Susan's outfit of choice helped her feel confident and professional, it was her mannerisms and outward confidence that lit up the room. The interview team was impressed, although her answers were similar to a few of the candidates. Her interview felt natural, and they were able to see how she could fit well into their school community.

LEARNING FROM SUSAN'S LEADERSHIP STORY

Susan's story spotlights a scenario that often causes anxiety. An interview process can shake confidence and amplify fear. Interviews can make a leader feel nervous or anxious, which then causes the brain's amygdala to have a fight, flight, or freeze response. When in a freeze state, it is very difficult to think clearly or present well in the interview.

Negative self-talk and inner dialogue then make it difficult to communicate. Similar to stage fright, a talented and prepared singer creates beautiful music in the privacy of a shower or car. Then when nerves and negative self-talk creep in, the singer is only able to squeak out an off-tune note. Nothing can be heard except shaking and cracking, no matter how hard the singer tries to relax. Like squeaking notes or chords, nerves make it difficult to think and process creative thoughts. This is a physiological fight, flight, or freeze response to the fear of an unfamiliar situation. When Susan's negative thoughts crept in, her body's natural response was to freeze until she was able to calm herself and take Nancy's advice to focus on being herself.

She was able to do so when she drowned out the negative thoughts by repeating, "The person who shows up for the job interview must be the person who will show up for work every day. Be yourself." Susan knew if she tried to be someone she was not, she would have to continue the false persona upon securing the job. She would also be more nervous in the interview if she tried to be someone she was not. Rather, if Susan were to be herself, she could hold her head high. If she was not a good fit for this particular job as her true self, it would be best she not land the position no matter how much she thought she wanted it.

When Susan prepared for her interview, her initial focus was on her attire. She planned her dress based on the message she wanted to send. She once read how fashion experts and political forum analysts assert the color blue sends a message of loyalty, reliability, and trust, while black and red suggest power and control. She remembered reading about the way aspiring politicians and presidential candidates carefully plan the color scheme of a wardrobe based on the message the party wants to send. A preoccupation with wardrobe made Susan forget appearances are much more than the right suit. Susan's confidence and poise did not derive from a color or a freshly pressed collar. Nancy taught her confidence came from a focus on her own skills and talents and the unique gifts that only she has.

Nancy's advice to Susan allowed her to be true to herself, which allowed her brain to think creatively rather than a flight or fight fear response from the amygdala. Being herself also allowed Susan to appear poised. Poised leaders are those who instantly gain trust. Poise includes taking up space rather than shrinking and hiding. Fidgeting and placing your hands under a table sends a message of insecurity, rather than confidence. It minimizes your presence and shrinks your confidence.[2] A strong posture, a genuine smile expressed with the face and eyes, and an attention to detail allow others to focus on a leader's skill set and experiences. It allows the leader to visually establish credibility.

A 2009 research study conducted at Ohio State University observed the confidence levels of seventy-one undergraduate students who were asked to change their posture from sitting up straight to sitting slouched forward facing their knees.[3] While directed to take the two different postures, the participants were asked to articulate their own positive and negative characteristics and their future potential success. The study showed the participants' body posture significantly affected their confidence levels, with those in upright posture being more confident in their responses about their perceived current and future success. So not only do posture and body language send a message to others about an individual's confidence, but it also affects one's self-attitude.

Much like interview scenarios, stressful meetings can shake confidence. Tips on posture and confidence can help when navigating those situations, but there is more to confidence than holding a strong posture. Women who hold positions at the top of an organizational chart, such as superintendents, are often the focus of challenges and attacks. Seasoned superintendents learn to let the emotions and frustrations roll off their backs like water off the back of a duck. It can be helpful to let the attacks roll off.

However, an empathetic and confident leader chooses to hear the attack and understand it but also works hard to not allow the attack to penetrate to a personal level. She uses armor, rather than the feathers of a duck's back. Unlike the back of a duck, which simply allows the issue to roll away, armor is a protective layer that may be removed during times the leader needs to lead with heart and sensitivity. Armor can be put back on during challenging times in which she needs to be callused. Most importantly, she is in control of when the armor is up or down, when she needs to feel the emotion of a situation, and when she needs to protect her heart from adversity or distress.

Confidence is critical for leaders who face challenging situations daily. Charisma and a strong presence help a leader gain the trust of those she leads. A confident leader is poised, trustworthy, flexible, and willing to show vulnerability and seek input from others. She is courageous, empathetic, and just.

However, confidence should not be confused with ego (see table 2.1). The two have very different influences on individuals and an organization. Ego presumes one is above, better than, or of greater value than a peer or colleague. Women in leadership positions often work hard to not appear arrogant, abrasive, or pushy. At the same time, they must find a balance when leading with kindness and thoughtfulness, which can be confused with weakness. An ego-driven leader is fueled by insecurity and fear and feels the need to be the smartest individual in the room. An ego-driven leader tells others how it must be done, is rigid and self-interested, and feels the need to display dominance.

Leadership requires courage and strength. However, I posit leaders of dynamic organizations should outwardly wear confidence and check their egos at the door. Confident leaders are empathetic leaders.

Table 2.1. Confidence versus Ego

Confidence looks like:	*Ego looks like:*
Poise	Arrogance
Owning space (body language: hands above table, strong posture)	Pushing (into a conversation or space)
Presence	Power
Engaging eye contact	Demanding attention
Active listening	Telling
Trustworthiness	Self-importance
Willingness to seek input or help	Feeling like the smartest person in the room
Flexible	Rigid
Confidence is borne of:	*Ego is borne of:*
Courage	Insecurity
Empathy	Underlying fear

Empathy is often defined as one's ability to relate to another's experiences or place oneself in the shoes of another. But it is actually about being able to hear the other's story about what it feels like to walk in their shoes. It is not possible to walk in someone else's shoes because we each have our own lens through which we view and experience situations. Rather, our efforts should be to honor someone else's perspective and value them for it.[4]

Ego-driven leaders do not lead with confident humility. Leaders who lead with their ego have an inflated sense of self and personal contributions. They take credit for group efforts, or even more unethically, they take credit for the efforts of others. Confident leaders, however, are those who allow others to receive the credit for success. They do not feel it is necessary to personally benefit from the success of a group. Rather, they most care about encouraging others. To inspire their colleagues and staff, a confident leader will allow the credit to be placed on those she leads. She takes these steps in a humble manner so they do not come across as condescending or fake.

Those who approach leadership wearing a big ego might subsequently subscribe to the "fake it till you make it" model, which implies one has to pretend. The approach may work well with low-level skills, such as managing protocols or outlining steps for a new set of paperwork. However, no one can or should feel compelled to fake their work. Using this common phrase implies one has no choice but to pretend. This, in turn, undervalues your skills and expertise and the unique gifts you bring to the work. While every leader has something to learn, it is not necessary to pretend while learning.

Effective leadership cannot be faked, but it can evolve and grow. You should be encouraged to promote what you do know while acquiring new knowledge or skills. We should replace the "fake it till you make it" phrase with "show it while you grow it." This change in the narrative highlights the skills the superintendent has while spotlighting a need to learn or grow additional skills. This adjusted lens is more than just a change in semantics. Having confidence and self-awareness honors that there will always be something to learn and skills to develop.

A confident leader is humble and recognizes there will always be more to learn. As leaders of learning organizations, thriving means you, too, must continue to learn and develop knowledge and skills. A leader's capacity to learn is dependent on her level of humility because she must be willing to recognize she does not and cannot know everything. She must be open to learning.

Inherent in leadership are humility and poise. For example, confident leaders do not feel it is necessary to blame others or throw them under the bus to prove their point. Poised leaders confidently walk into a room and graciously interact with colleagues and staff. They keep calm when tensions rise in a room and do not let emotions control reactions. This is possible when a leader doesn't put herself and her sense of self above others. She is respectful of others' opinions and input, even when the immediate reaction is to dismiss the idea. Leadership skills such as poise and confidence can be cultivated and grown.

SWIMMING WITH CONFIDENCE

Leadership confidence resembles personal confidence but is unique because it requires competence and skills, in addition to empathy and understanding.

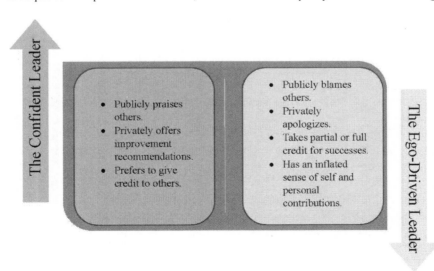

People follow decisive individuals who feel comfortable sharing their point of view while also being respectful of others' opinions. They follow leaders who do not feel it necessary to be seen as the smartest person in the room. They follow leaders who are courageous and portray a level of confidence without being abrasive. This requires a leader to be confident and calm while also selecting the moments in which she must be assertive.

Leading with confidence requires resourcefulness as well as competence and empathy. Too little empathy and a high level of competence create an arrogant, controlling leader who can float through daily tasks but doesn't leave a positive ripple effect on the organization. Conversely, an empathetic leader who has a low level of competence is caring but will struggle to take the organization forward.

There are four quadrants within which leaders can be categorized. And there are lessons to move from one quadrant to another, toward the goal of becoming a confident leader.

THE CONFIDENT LEADER: SWIMMING

Swimming requires you to trust in your skills, to be confident that you will not sink below the surface of deep water. Learning to swim means taking small steps and remaining calm in turbulent waters. A leader who wishes to swim confidently must first reflect on her core values prior to taking on a new challenge or intimidating waters. She must bravely take the first step and own

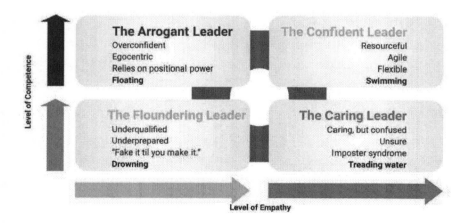

her confidence. She must also keep her emotions in control so as not to cause panic during the swim.

A confident leader is one who is resourceful and agile and will slide through the water toward her organization's goals, knowing she can steer around obstacles by being flexible and seeking support from colleagues, research, or outside sources. Much like a strong swimmer, she is agile and able to navigate rough waters or adversity. Building this type of strength in swimming requires practice and endurance. Swimming requires a leader to be calm and steady, with a smooth and strategic stroke. Similarly, leadership also requires agility, practice, endurance, and a sense of calm.

Confident leadership also requires rehearsal and learning from experience, and there are many ways to exercise the muscles necessary for leadership, much like swimming. The confident leader is determined, able to pivot when necessary, and approaches situations with grace and empathy for those she leads.

As a leader, when engaging in a challenging situation or meeting, you should intentionally notice your body posture, eye contact, gaze, and movement as well as tone and intonation of voice. Posture and the way a leader uses space send a message of confidence or insecurity and doubt.

THE CARING LEADER: TREADING WATER

Treading water takes a lot of effort but creates no progress forward. It is an excellent survival skill because it allows a swimmer to keep their head above water until help arrives or turbulent waters pass. But when treading water, a swimmer remains in one place. A leader who is caring but does not have the skills necessary for the position is treading water. She is working hard but does not have the skills to make decisions and move the organization forward. She needs help or support—a lifeline.

It goes without saying that everyone wants a leader who is caring. Caring leaders are empathetic and well liked. However an empathetic leader who has a low level of competence and knowledge will only be well liked for a short period of time because the team will not respect her.

A caring leader is treading water, staying in one place, until such time when others realize she does not have the necessary skills to lead and set a vision for the organization. She is able to keep her chin above water, but under the water, she has to work very hard to appear in control. As she treads water, she does not make any movement forward. Her effort keeps the organization from drowning, but it also remains stagnant year after year.

The caring leader is plagued with the imposter syndrome. She realizes she needs to improve her skill set because she is in tune with the feelings of others. A caring leader treads water while searching for answers to her lack of competence. What this leader needs is a mentor. She needs someone whom she can trust to learn the skills and find the resources to turn treading water into a strong swimmer's stroke. Much like a swim instructor, a mentor can offer suggestions and solutions to help her move forward with progress rather than stand still in her work.

Some women fall into the Caring Leader quadrant because they want to be liked but lack the confidence to fight for a seat at the table. In an attempt to be respectful, many women respond to praise, acknowledgment, or compliments by completely deferring credit to others or even uttering self-deprecating replies. They think agreeing with the praise will come across as arrogant or self-righteous. Their cultural norms have told them to humbly discount compliments as a sign of respectfulness.

Almost automatically, women push back in response to a compliment. A peer states, "I am so impressed with how you presented that information." Then the leader replies, "I was simply presenting what the others on the team worked hard to create." Or a colleague offers, "Wow, what a great article you published." She replies, "Oh, it was nothing. Just a little idea I had. I am sure you could have done better. But thank you."

From early ages, girls are taught to sit back from the table, to shrink down and use a soft voice.[5] They are told it is polite to be modest and demure as a matter of etiquette. Young girls are encouraged to be respectful of others' voices, meek and reticent. Years later, as women in leadership roles, they receive a mixed message and are expected to have a strong voice and powerful stance.

Women are often led to believe they should be more aggressive, rather than humble and empathetic. Humility is a positive character trait for a leader, but it should not overshadow confidence and self-assurance. There must be a balance between being humble and remaining confident. A leader should be humble but not self-deprecating. Self-deprecating comments only serve to publicly downgrade respect and negatively affect a woman's personal confidence level. While building competence, those in the Caring Leader quadrant should also practice accepting compliments and praise. Leaders should inspire confidence in one another and give ourselves and one another permission to be prideful when we achieve.

THE ARROGANT LEADER: FLOATING

Consider the last time you floated on your back in a lake or pool or sank into a tub to relax. Your ears were underwater, creating a peaceful silence, leaving you unobservant to the world. You only heard your own breath. Floating is a peaceful experience. The rest of the world is silenced and only your thoughts penetrate the silence.

Similarly, an arrogant leader silences all but her own thoughts and desires. It's as if she is floating on her back with her eyes closed and ears under water so she cannot hear. She is unmindful of the outside world. Because she is overconfident, she is not open to learning from others, especially those she leads. She will, therefore, be misguided and not accepted by her team.

An arrogant leader has a high level of competence and skill. She is well read and resourceful, likely experienced, and held in high regard for her knowledge. However, she is not in touch with the needs of her team, and therefore makes decisions that do not support them. She demands and commands respect. Her low self-awareness and arrogance stand in the way of her leadership because she is closed off and believes only her ideas are of merit.

The arrogant leader relies on her positional power to dominate and direct others. She is more interested in being the boss than supporting and encouraging others. She is forceful and quick to respond based on what she knows and believes to be the best. The arrogant leader believes she is and must continue to be the smartest person in the room. She does not actively listen. Rather, she listens to be able to respond because she wants to have the last word in a discussion. When challenged on an idea, she turns to her positional authority and expects her team to respect her.

Because the arrogant leader is low in the area of self-awareness, she would benefit from a critical, trusted mentor. This should be a mentor who is willing to call out ways in which the leader is acting in a self-centered manner. Much like holding up a mirror, the mentor should point out areas in need of improvement in a very clear manner. Unfortunately, by nature, an arrogant leader is not likely to be receptive to the idea of working with a critical counterpart.

THE FLOUNDERING LEADER: DROWNING

Drowning is scary. It is a fight for stability in the water. While energy is expended, it is not helpful to the situation. Rather, it makes matters worse because all movement of arms and legs is reactionary and responsive to fear. A floundering leader who is drowning needs the support of her colleagues who are confidently swimming. When drowning, an individual will often panic and react in an overly aggressive manner, flailing arms and splashing aggressively. This reaction worsens the situation, only creating more panic and an exponentially more difficult situation. Similarly, a floundering leader lacks the level of competence or empathy necessary for her role. She is truly in over her head and may not recognize it.

A floundering leader is underqualified for her position and should consider taking a new position for which her skills are better aligned. A floundering leader is not only detrimental to the organization but also to her own professional growth and self. Because she is drowning, she will pull down those around her but also do harm to her own career. While floundering feels like a failure, it does not have to be. When the leader recognizes she is floundering and not a good fit for her current role, she is doing herself and the organization a service and is being respectful of both by moving on. A floundering leader who makes a significant role change may find herself swimming elsewhere.

MOVING BETWEEN THE QUADRANTS

Leader effectiveness and ability to support the organization is dependent on the quadrant. It is possible to evolve from one quadrant to another. To progress from one quadrant to the next, you should make use of mentoring, goal setting, and possibly a personal development plan or professional improvement plan.

For example, to develop skills in empathy and become a more empathetic leader, you should employ questioning strategies as a personal development goal. When approaching a staff member conflict or a parent concern, it is wise to approach by first identifying the other's perspective.

Building empathy requires you to put yourself in the shoes of another, not with a goal of replicating their experience but to better understand how they respond and react based on those experiences.[6] You can build a level of empathy by reflecting on the following questions about the individual you are meeting with or talking to:

- What is this individual's motivation?
- What is the individual's situation?
- How is this individual feeling at this moment given the situation?
- Perceived or real, what is the individual's lens?

Empathy is a skill that can be learned and developed. Many women are naturally empathetic. Although this is a strength in leadership, some may misunderstand it as a weakness, as a leader who is too soft. But the most effective leaders are those who are empathetic. Empathetic leaders are kind and considerate and skilled in building relationships. When they model empathy a strong culture can be established throughout the organization.

An illustration of the application of empathy in leadership is a leader who receives a phone call from a parent who is upset over a leadership decision.

While phone calls with angry parents can begin with frustration and emotion, a skilled leader can help resolve the situation by using empathic language, such as "I understand you are upset and frightened and you disagree with our decision to . . ."

You should be cautious to use language that comes across sincerely and not condescending. Next, you can say, "We are going to do everything in our power to . . . ," ensuring promises made are promises kept. Throughout the conversation, you should listen to understand and allow quiet moments to provide deeper consideration, even when those pauses in the conversation feel awkward. The silence of an awkward pause can provide the encouragement for the other individual to reflect and provide more detail on the original thought, going deeper into the topic, rather than remaining on the surface. To wrap up the conversation, seek clarification by saying, "Is there anything we can give you to help you ease your fears/concerns?" Most importantly, you should follow through with any promises made in the conversation.

Advancement within the quadrants toward the top right corner requires high levels of empathy. Swimming confidently as a leader also calls for an increase in competence and skills. Some skills are acquired with time and years of experience in a career. Competence is built with experience, growing knowledge and skills. Growth in the area of competence is also possible through the support of an experienced mentor, professional association, conferences, or literature.

While the leader's goal is to function in the top right corner, there are times that empathy must be dialed back. There are times callused and calculated responses are needed, and others that call for softer, more empathetic responses.

For example, during a public meeting in which a parent angrily yells at the superintendent and her board of education, a shield of armor allows the superintendent to remain composed and professional and not to inappropriately roll her eyes or smirk. But when the parent then breaks down with emotion and explains her child is struggling academically, the superintendent can then pull down the armor and empathize with the parent. She can put herself in the mother's shoes and see how she is coming from a place of concern and frustration. The two can then have a conversation about working together to find solutions. The shield of armor allows you to be strong and poised yet empathetic, intuitive, and nurturing.

LEADERSHIP TIPS

- A confident leader has a high level of empathy and competence. She is resourceful, agile, and flexible.

- Build your level of empathy by being curious about another person's perspective.
- A quick boost of confidence comes with shoulders back, head high, hands above the table, and eye contact.
- Be true to yourself. The person who shows up for the interview must show up for the job every day. That perspective can be applied to many stressful situations, not only an interview.
- Movement toward the top right corner of the confidence quadrant is achieved through empathy, personal reflection, support from a mentor, and the courage to move forward.

Chapter 3

Keychains

Women in leadership say they fear "Failing as a working mother with not enough time in a day."

Leadership roles are demanding of time, energy, and emotion. All day, every day, leaders are expected to make decisions that have a direct influence on the lives of hundreds or even thousands. Women in leadership express a strong sense of responsibility for their role. Most find it difficult to turn the work off at night. They check emails every two or three minutes on a never-out-of-reach cellular phone. They step away from family time to make work calls more often than they realize. And the phone calls they accept outside of work hours require immediate attention and often have a negative effect on emotions, resulting in frustration, fear, or anger.

Because they often take their work home, the best keychain a leader carries is a valet-style keychain. The valet keychain has a detachable keyring that is easily removed or disconnected. At the end of a workday or workweek, being able to physically detach work keys from car and home keys is a symbolic action representative of the detachment between the tethers of work to sacred home priorities. The motion can indicate a release of the attachment to stress and work pressures. While valet keychains are useful for the luxury of valet parking, perhaps more salient, valet keyrings help leaders prioritize and compartmentalize.

TISHA'S LEADERSHIP STORY

As a school principal, Tisha felt she found her dream job. It was a career she felt provided her with the ability to lead while also still serving in the teaching role. Only now she was a teacher of teachers and loved being able to inspire and encourage her staff. Because she believed this was her dream job, she spent many hours dedicated to the work. She enjoyed impressing others with her creativity and ability to build relationships. Tisha felt happy in classrooms, observing and coaching teachers, or in the cafeteria giving high-fives to students throughout the day. She left most of her paperwork responsibilities for the hours after or before school.

Tisha found herself working late hours every evening. She would return to school on the weekends to complete reports or evaluations. Her husband was very supportive of her professional goals and never complained about the hours she spent. Rather, he would find ways to support her. He would bring a coffee or a lunch to her when she would work weekends. He was proud of her and enjoyed seeing her thrive in the role.

Five years into her position as a school principal, Tisha began to question her decision to be the leader. Working late nights often meant she did not have dinner with her family. Her children were active in sports, and she missed many events. While her husband continued to be supportive of her, he, too, began to feel the job was prioritized over their family. They tried to carve out quality time for vacations or trips to see extended family members, but even those were often interrupted when a staff member called or the building had a facility emergency such as a malfunctioning alarm system or a leaky faucet. Tisha began to feel tired and wished there were more hours in a day.

Two years before her oldest daughter was scheduled to go to college, Tisha realized she had given up many precious memories. She could not get them back. Tisha was proud she had climbed professionally but realized it came at a high cost because soon her daughter would be gone from the home and beginning her independent life.

As a Christmas present, Tisha's daughter gave her a precious gift. Tisha opened a small box with a teal bow to find a valet-style keychain. Her daughter explained how she thought it was a keychain her mom could use for both home and work keys. Tisha thought it was a beautiful gift and quickly attached her work, house, and car keys to it.

Two weeks later as she drove home from work on a Friday night, Tisha unclicked her work keys from the keychain and set them in the glove compartment of her SUV. She promised herself she would keep the office keys in the car and spend the weekend with her family. Unless there was an emergency, she would not go back into the office and would focus on giving her undivided attention to her family.

Because she took an intentional step to detach, Tisha enjoyed the weekend with her family and also found herself setting aside her cell phone to focus on conversations with her children. It was not until then that she wondered when the last time she read them a bedtime story was or the last time they asked her to sing a lullaby before delaying bedtime by "one more minute." Her children had grown up in what felt like a flash and now were teenagers who did not need her like they had ten years ago. Bittersweet emotions filled her heart. Tisha was proud they had developed into independent teens but longed for the days she knew had slipped away too quickly while she was focused on her career.

After detaching and spending the weekend with her family, Tisha returned to work on Monday morning feeling refreshed and positive. She ritualized the process of removing her work keys every afternoon and weekend. The physical detachment of her work keys served as a reset and a reminder to disconnect from work to prioritize herself and her family. Not only was she a better mother and wife; Tisha became a better school leader. She vowed to ask her staff to also find rituals they could use to step away from work and prioritize their families and friends outside the workday.

LEARNING FROM TISHA'S LEADERSHIP STORY

Tisha felt tethered to her work. There is a difference between a tether that fastens or secures and a tether that anchors and weighs down. Tethers can secure us to our priorities, such as family and friends, and help focus on the most important aspects of our work. But tethers can also drag down our energy and tear us from the work. Tethers can heavily weigh down even the most skilled or experienced leader. They pull attention from priorities, add pressure, and do not allow forward movement.

There are times to intentionally compartmentalize family and home from work to fully care for each. A leader must reflect on those moments and ask herself, "To what specifically am I tethered, and why? Am I tethered to email because I want to please? Do I feel tethered to email because there is not enough time in the day to answer them? Or is the tether present because I am afraid an email might slide to the bottom of my inbox, where I will later forget to address it?" No matter the reason for the tether, it most likely interferes with connections to family and friends.

Research suggests the ability to detach from job stress and care for family or friends allows a leader the opportunity to return to work fully engaged and recharged. Especially when dealing with challenging situations, a fresh perspective is valuable. Leaders who can physically remove their work keys from their personal car keys or house keys are leaders who can pause the work, go home and enjoy family, then return in the morning to tackle the challenge with a fresh outlook. A valet keychain can serve as a whimsical, novel reminder of the need to detach and compartmentalize stressful situations from the joy of life.

A leader's family and friends deserve her full attention. They are not part of the boardroom stress, so they cannot relate to or empathize with the pain it causes. Therefore, when the pain spills over into her home, it damages the most valuable relationships.

Tethers that tie us to our work can also be weighted with anchors. Obstructive anchors are those that pull down a leader as she attempts to guide the organization. Sadly, sometimes the anchors that hold women down are other women. Women are anchored by colleagues, peers, employees, or perhaps even board members. This results in feelings of defensiveness and fear. Real or perceived, we are plagued with competition and jealousy. Women in leadership report feeling fear that if one woman is successful or does well it somehow means there are fewer seats at the table. They mistakenly believe when one woman rises, it must be on the backs of others.

DETACHING

Detaching our keys is symbolic of our boundaries. As leaders, we must set our own boundaries for our leadership roles. Some women report they must work out every day for an hour; others turn off their phones every Sunday morning for church and family. Others make it a priority to pick their children up at school, even if it means they must go back to the office for an evening meeting.

Leaders should set boundaries. If social media comments sting personally, a leader might set a boundary to not monitor it due to the negative, toxic posts and their effect on the leader's mental health. A leader who sets a boundary to not view social media might instead ask a staff member to let her know if information is posted on which she should react.

Whatever your boundaries are, set them in line with your beliefs and core values. Then articulate them to your team and your board members. Tell them, "This is how I am at my best. I need these boundaries in order to be fully engaged and the best leader I can be."

LEADERSHIP TIPS

- The valet-style keychain reminds leaders of the importance of prioritizing family, friends, faith, and self.
- A daily ritual such as unhooking office keys can provide the opportunity to release the stress of work life for a healthy balance.
- Establish boundaries and articulate them to supervisors and colleagues.

Chapter 4

Self-Care and Surrogate Stress

Women in leadership say they fear "Not being able to endure the stress of the leadership position."

Women in leadership wear many hats—mother, wife, sister, friend, daughter, community leader. They carry responsibilities such as managing households, managing relationships, and coordinating childcare in addition to work-related responsibilities.[1] The compounded pressures can feel overwhelming. If not mitigated, the pressures can affect a leader's overall health and wellness and result in burnout.

Women in leadership often take on the role of caregivers. They want to support and uplift those around them, but to be ready to care for others, they must first take care of themselves. It is common that women put others before themselves and then neglect their own needs.[2]

ERICA'S LEADERSHIP STORY

Erica's burnout happened during the COVID-19 pandemic. Erica was the superintendent of a school district with eight schools and over five thousand students. Every day, she faced the challenges of determining which public health safety protocols she would recommend, which she would require, and which she would consider but eventually dismiss.

In between reading email blast updates from the local health department, Erica was inundated with phone calls and emails from staff members at all levels of her organization. Individuals from every category of positions were repeatedly reaching out to Erica to tell her they could not handle one more stressor.

Teachers, support staff, directors, and building principals were frustrated and exhausted. They met their personal limit, and one after another they reached out to Erica to tell her they were at a breaking point. Erica held a lot of respect for each of them. She wanted to fix their issues, to rejuvenate them, and to help them refocus their energy. She tried to pour her positivity and creative solutions into their concerns, but with each phone call and interaction, Erica felt more and more defeated.

As their school district leader, Erica did her best to support them, spending many hours every day brainstorming solutions or support. She revised schedules, added resources, and sent staff emails. But the concerns just kept coming. While none of the individuals expected Erica to fix all of their stressors, she felt obligated to them to try. It weighed heavily on her when she received calls from staff who were at their breaking point, saying "I am drowning" or "I am overwhelmed." As their leader, she wanted to fix everything. She wanted to promise their concerns would soon be better. But she could not.

While washing her hair in the shower one morning, Erica noticed a handful of hair fell from her head. That had never happened to her before, and she knew it was a symptom of the stress she experienced. Her body was sending her a message. She had to slow down. Erica began to cry and felt herself fall apart. Later the same morning, she called her general practitioner and made an appointment, fearing she could not cope with the issues alone any longer.

Erica explained to her physician how she had always been able to handle stress but what she experienced lately was unique. From budget reductions to terminations of staff, she always had the skills and courage in the past to make tough decisions for the organization. Leading through the pandemic was unlike any challenge Erica had faced in the past. She did not have solutions to the issues she faced, and the constant barrage of concerns and questions was weighing heavily on her.

Erica knew she could not take time off to rest and reset because the staff needed her to rally. She didn't feel comfortable being honest with her staff about the fact that she was at her breaking point. She thought this type of honesty and candor would come across as a sign of vulnerability and weakness from their leader. Erica thought it was her responsibility to endure and to be strong for them.

After a discussion of her current work pressures and health, Erica's doctor prescribed medication for the anxiety symptoms and panic attacks. Erica was grateful to have a tool to combat anxiety, but she also committed to making lifestyle and health changes to help her cope. She turned to meditation, breathing exercises, yoga, and journaling her gratitude daily.

She realized she could no longer try to fix all of the issues her staff brought to her. Rather, she needed to see herself as a therapist might see herself, someone who could ask individuals the questions they could use to come up with solutions. Shifting the problem solving back would allow Erica to encourage and support them as they followed through with the solutions.

A few weeks later, Erica attended a meeting of area school district leaders hosted by the health department. During a coffee break, Erica approached Olivia, a colleague in a neighboring school district. The two exchanged pleasantries and small talk. Olivia asked how Erica was handling the stress.

Erica paused and asked Olivia if it was typical to work from early in the morning to very late at night. Olivia told her not only was it atypical; it was unhealthy and unsustainable. She encouraged Erica to find a balance by delegating to building leaders or encouraging staff to play a more significant role in the planning and administration of protocols. Olivia was not aware of Erica's visit to her doctor, but she could see the effects the stress was having on her health. Even if Erica tried to maintain this strenuous schedule, it was not possible to sustain it, and she would find herself looking for a way out of the leadership role if nothing changed.

Olivia reached into her pocket and pulled out a small plastic button. She handed it to Erica and began to tell her a story. She asked her to look at the four thread holes on the button. Olivia explained how each symbolized a priority in life. One represents self, another represents family, the third represents friends, and the fourth work/career ambitions. Self, family, friends, work. She explained how each must be threaded and tended to for the button to remain secured. The ability to thread each in a balanced way helps maintain balance in life.

Olivia asked Erica to notice how work was a single thread hole of four. She illustrated how if only it was threaded, the button would certainly fall off. While work life is significant, it is just one part of life, and the other three pieces deserve attention and care. Olivia shared how she, too, cares a great deal about her career goals but only threading the work section of the button would make it hang unbalanced or become unfastened and fall off completely.

Erica placed the button in her pocket as a reminder to balance each priority in her life. She recognized that when her hair fell out a few weeks before, she had not been caring for herself. She was not threading the "self" hole in the button, and it became unfastened and fell off. Each time she placed her hand in her pocket, she would feel a reminder to take care of herself, her family, her friends, and her work.

LEARNING FROM ERICA'S LEADERSHIP STORY

Erica lost sight of her own self-care and found herself in an unhealthy situation. Caring for self includes balanced nutrition, regular exercise, and proper sleep. Each is elemental in overall health and wellness, especially in high-pressure work environments. Nutrition can provide or drain energy.

Specifically, proper nutrition shifts the focus from eating for entertainment or comfort to eating for fuel. Fuel of a balanced diet sustains an otherwise stressed body. These tools can be used to navigate stress even as the pandemic becomes a distant memory.

One of the most stressful seasons in the career cycle of contemporary leaders was the COVID-19 pandemic. Protocols changed daily, structures and procedures required multiple redesigns, staff and parents were stressed, and students struggled to engage in learning. The pandemic confiscated a significant level of energy from educators, but it also drew attention to the need for mindfulness and meditation. Educators engaged in yoga, meditation, and calming techniques, which were previously only used in schools for students as a tool to curtail behavior outbursts and student stress levels, all in the name of self-care.

The pandemic marked a unique challenge for leaders because every individual within our organization faced new and stressful changes. We were inundated with questions about navigating the changes but did not have access to the answers or success models to emulate because the pandemic was novel. It created a microcosm in which to analyze the importance of caring for one's self.

Research on the benefits of exercise and self-care techniques has been widely embraced throughout the pandemic, and, more recently, through the pandemic recovery phase. Gratitude journals and yoga are proven to be able to help improve mental and physical health. Daily exercise such as a brisk walk has many health benefits. Using a standing desk, in comfy shoes, is also a heart-healthy practice to adopt. Each of these practices are small steps that can be helpful in reducing stress and improving health. However, addressing burnout must go beyond deep breathing, meditation, or going for a walk. To better address burnout, we must better understand the elements of a healthy work environment.

The Office of the Surgeon General identified five essentials for workplace mental health and well-being.[3] The Surgeon General's framework identifies the following as necessary to a healthy work environment: protection from harm, connection and community, work–life harmony, matter at work, and opportunity for growth. Taken together, these areas support a positive work environment. Specifically, the Surgeon General describes work–life harmony as the balance of the ability to be autonomous and flexible. Employees are most successful when they are able to control the way in which they complete tasks, with flexible scheduling.[4] Not only does this create a mutual trusting relationship, but it also allows individuals to balance their work with necessary rest periods.

Throughout the pandemic, many stresses landed on the shoulders of leaders who found it difficult to rest or balance. Similar to a secondary trauma, leaders felt cumulative stress while they attempted to support students, staff, and families who were also under pressure. I refer to it as a surrogate stress. Leaders were directly affected by the stress of others but were unable to resolve the cause of the stress.

SURROGATE STRESS AND THE LUCY EFFECT

Surrogate stress can be illustrated by my own canine. I have two dogs who are both loving, sweet, and full of personality. Rosie is a cream-colored doodle mix who is obsessed with chasing tennis balls. She is a clumsy but sweet dog with lots of spunk. No matter what mood you bring to the room, Rosie's personality is constant. She wants to love and snuggle and play cheerfully. My second dog, Lucy, is quite different from Rosie. While she, too, is a doodle mix and loving, she prefers to stand back and cautiously observe a situation. Lucy is sensitive and can read the room, including feeling the emotions of a situation. We've always thought Lucy would make a terrific therapy dog if only we had trained her beyond the few cute tricks she does for a treat reward.

If two people in the house are having a debate, Lucy interjects herself. She will come up and paw at one person to make the debate or argument stop. If a ball game is on the television and someone yells in excitement, Lucy will insert herself. We find ourselves saying, with a sing-song intonation, "Lucy, we're not mad. We're just yelling at the television. Everyone is OK."

Lucy feels even the smallest amount of stress in a room. She knows it is not directed at her, but she senses it and wants it to stop. It is not her stress, but it becomes her stress, a surrogate stress. Surrogate stress is felt by someone near who is empathetic like Lucy is. While Rosie is unaware of the stress in a room, Lucy feels it and internalizes it.

Sometimes this type of secondary, surrogate stress is even more detrimental because like Lucy, a person who absorbs it from being nearby has no ability to change or control it. Lucy doesn't feel in control of our stress levels. She feels the energy, but she doesn't have the tools to decrease it because she was never trained as an emotional support animal. She tries to help, but likely feels helpless.

Leaders want to fix issues or help alleviate concerns and may feel helpless to do so. Sometimes the best way to help someone is to coach the individual to resolve the problem on their own and to recognize that not every issue is within the influence of the leader. Perhaps Lucy's action of pawing at us is her way of coaching us to decrease our own stress.

The staff members and students we lead feel the stress we carry, and we internalize theirs. Our own families feel the pressures we carry. Even when we try to mask our stress, it is often projected onto others. Part of being strong means finding a way to compartmentalize stress so it does not spill onto those around us. This means there must be a counterbalance between taking care of the organization and taking care of self.

PILY: PEOPLE INSIDE LOVE YOU

Ten years ago, during a stressful and challenging season of my career, I was fortunate to attend a presentation by author and highly respected retired superintendent Jim Burgett. In a room full of hundreds of school superintendents, Jim highlighted the need for leaders to take care of themselves. He gave an inspiring and powerful presentation that captured the attention of the hard-working officials. Jim, who was also a former Illinois Superintendent of the Year, told the story of his career and its influence on his family.

Jim told stories of days he would arrive at home from a challenging board meeting and holding on to the frustration, would shrug off the affection of his wife and children because he was preoccupied with the work. We could all relate to the stress he described.

Jim praised his wife for the way she reminded him that she and his children were not privy to the struggles of work and deserved for him to release them before he stepped in the door. She placed a sticky note on the doorframe from their garage to their home that read "PILY." This note served as a simple but cardinal reminder: "People Inside Love You." She asked him to remember this as he stepped into their home where his family was eagerly awaiting his arrival. The people inside were the most important in his life, and they deserved his attention, love, and happiness. The note served as a powerful visual reminder for Jim and forever after, for all of the leaders with whom he shared his story.

After the presentation, I walked up to the front of the conference ballroom to say hello. Jim attentively and genuinely asked how I was doing. Unexpectedly, I broke into tears. I was embarrassed at first because I assumed my emotions made me look weak. I didn't mean to become so emotional, but I was feeling very vulnerable because I knew his presentation message was one I needed to hear. I, too, had been putting my work over family, and they were what mattered most to me.

Jim's response helped me see there was no reason to be ashamed of my reaction to his message. It was OK that I allowed the message to help me reflect on my priorities. Jim asked a few more questions about the stress of my job. I explained how our school district had some troubling news about theft from a retired employee who many in the organization had trusted. I bore the stress because I could not tell the staff we were investigating the matter with authorities. While that story is now in the public record, very few people were aware of it at the time of the investigation. I felt very isolated in the stress from the situation and the weight of the matter.

Jim's message provided an important reminder to me. While my family is not privy to the details of my stress, they feel the ripple emotions when I bring frustrations or anger into our relationships through the door to our home. They feel a surrogate stress of the emotions I bring home.

I went home and also put a note on the door to my garage to remind myself to let go of stress to the best of my ability at the end of the day. My sign at the door is still there today; it reads, "The place to be happy is here. The time to be happy is now." My intentional step to remind myself and my family of this priority is a constant reminder to prioritize those who love me.

LEADERSHIP TIPS

- Control what you can control. It's harmful to stress about what you cannot.
- Equally tend to priorities of work, family, self, and friends.
- Keep a single button in your pocket as a reminder but also to share the story with others who may need it.
- PILY: Be present with those you love.

Chapter 5

Time as a Precious Resource

Women in leadership say they fear "Failing as a working mother with not enough time in a day."

Many female leaders carry a specific type of guilt, a working-mom guilt. They express concerns about losing time with their own children as a result of the time-intensive demands of their executive leadership role. The guilt is compounded when they dedicate time to their families and subsequently feel they aren't providing enough time or energy to work priorities. It is a cycle of never feeling able to give enough time to both their family and their career ambitions.

ANN'S LEADERSHIP STORY

Ann was the only central office administrator in her small school district. As the superintendent, she wore many hats. She had two principals in her district who were effective leaders and building managers. Ann was the superintendent but also filled the roles of the district's business manager, human resource director, technology coordinator, curriculum director, social media content director, and policy director. Districts larger than hers had individuals in each of those roles, but in a school district of four hundred students, Ann did it all.

Ann tried to keep it all organized but often felt overwhelmed. She was grateful that many of her teachers and her two principals helped in other areas, such as website development or truancy compliance meetings. Still Ann often felt like a circus performer, balancing thirty spinning plates all at once while acting calm and in control. Ann thought she was expected to be all to everyone.

From the first day in her leadership position, Ann maintained an open door policy. She told her administrators, teachers, and staff her door was always open to them. Her secretary knew she never wanted to turn a staff member away when they came with a concern. She learned that when an employee asked to talk to her, sometimes there was more to the request than what appeared on the surface. Ann had experiences with staff who began to share a concern about a specific matter, but as they began to dig into the issue, she would hear the staff member was also battling a family struggle or personal health concern. Ann chose to never deny a staff member who asked to meet and to make it a priority in her schedule.

One afternoon five teachers met in the conference room outside Ann's office to align curriculum and update their scope and sequence. Two of the teachers asked to meet with her during a break and explained their concerns. Ann had a full schedule that day, with last-minute preparations for the evening's board meeting. She also needed to return a call to a board member and prepare a newsletter she would send to parents at the end of the week. But Ann could see in the teachers' body language that they needed her attention, so she agreed to meet within the hour.

The teachers stepped into Ann's office just as she finished her call with the board member who was upset about the evening's board meeting agenda. Throughout their twenty-minute phone call, he expressed his anger toward Ann about the item not being included on the agenda.

When the teachers began to talk to Ann, she felt very distracted and pulled in many directions. She explained she had just finished a high-priority phone call and she had a few other meetings she needed to get to soon. Ann did not realize how unimportant this made the two of them feel. Ann thought it was polite to apologize for her distraction, but the underlying, more sustaining message it sent was they were not as valued as the other items to which she needed to attend.

The teachers respected Ann, so they continued to share their concerns, knowing she would help them process through each. Ann's phone buzzed, and she reacted by glancing at the incoming call, grimacing, and then turning the phone over. She did not realize she also glanced at her clock on the wall even as she tried hard to focus on them.

The teachers thanked her for her time, and she again apologized for how busy her day was. They felt her genuine remorse, and they respected her busy schedule. If only Ann had been able to reset her thoughts and dedicate the few minutes they requested, they would have felt valued, and Ann would have actually saved the time she spent asking them to repeat several statements when her mind wandered. She wouldn't have felt it necessary to explain her day and apologize for the items on her plate.

LEARNING FROM ANN'S LEADERSHIP STORY

While her own distractions were significant to Ann, they were not significant to the two teachers who visited her that day. They did not need to hear the details of Ann's distractions. They only needed to hear she respected and appreciated them and to know that her full attention was theirs for their entire conversation. If Ann could not provide them her attention for the full ten minutes, she should have rescheduled their conversation to a time that she would be able to fully attend to their concerns.

Ann's leadership story provides an example of the need to establish boundaries, such as limiting the number of distractions in her day by delegating tasks to her secretary or rescheduling meetings to a less stressful time. Ann would have then been able to focus on the issue at hand but also balance her own stress levels. Because she felt pulled in so many directions, she doubted her own abilities. She was under a great deal of pressure as an accomplished and hardworking leader. She worried about failing her colleagues and her family, when in reality, she was an outstanding leader who was simply overscheduled, overcommitted, and overwhelmed.

The most successful leaders are those who establish boundaries but are also able to compartmentalize, or divide, their attention. While the leader may have ten significant issues to juggle immediately prior to stepping into a meeting with a small group of employees, she must take a moment to recognize they are not privy to the same information. They do not know she is balancing back-to-back meetings, nor should they. It is not within their sphere of control and should not interrupt her attention with them.

Before stepping into a meeting, she should turn her phone upside down and give her undivided attention to the group in front of her because they may only need ten minutes of her full attention, but those ten minutes are important to them. If she spends eight of the ten minutes explaining how she has some very significant people waiting for her after the meeting or how she has many things on her mind, the message they receive is that they are not a priority for her time. Instead of being distracted and making excuses for the many interruptions or issues she must attend to, the leader should dedicate those minutes solely to the group and allow them to receive her time and attention.

Ann is not alone in feeling overcommitted, overscheduled, and overwhelmed. While at work, women in leadership stress about their own children's success and well-being or the household tasks yet to be completed. When at home, female leaders worry there is a school event at which they should be present or a budget to balance. All of those activities demand and deserve attention, which makes a balance difficult to achieve. The women recognize it is hard work to achieve a leadership position, and they feel fearful it will be taken away or their contribution will be diminished when they spend time prioritizing family, self, and friends. They fear being replaced when others step in to cover when they are not present at work. Even though this fear is most often a misguided one, women in leadership fret over it.

Some female superintendents report a feeling of mom guilt when they miss their own children's ball games to attend sporting events for students in their schools. Female superintendents often report carrying the guilt of knowing we spend more time supporting the academic success of other people's children than our own. One superintendent said she felt a pit in her stomach when she realized she spent years of her career making sure students could read but then did not recognize when her own daughter was a struggling reader. When her daughter's teacher pointed out the concerns, she questioned herself as a mother for not seeing it sooner. Her mom guilt troubled her and made her question if she had placed too much emphasis on her career goals.

The panacea for working-mom guilt begins with the recognition of the merit of the work being done. Women at the top of their careers are passionate about their work and recognize how important it is. The mom who is working full-time and taking graduate-degree courses may miss her daughter's basketball games or cheerleading practices. However, as she spends evenings typing on her laptop from the home office, what she models for her young daughter is the way in which her computer is a gateway to professional growth and self-empowerment, rather than merely a tool for entertainment. As a mother, she models the importance of learning and achievement and self-worth.

However, the guilt of spending many hours at work and not being able to attend to family still pulls on the hearts of women in leadership. They also recognize the same is true for those who work for them. Staff also feel pressures of balancing work and home priorities. Leaders must maintain a strong sense of social awareness. There are times when staff are dealing with significant life events or media influences.

Valuing staff time also means not sending important messages on a Friday evening when staff should be with their families and friends or not expecting the team to take work on vacation trips. Conscientious staff who want to impress their leader and are loyal to the mission will be the first to bring stacks of work on a family vacation or open emails all hours of the evening. The leader needs to communicate how critical it is that they check out and immerse themselves in moments with family and friends.

During the pandemic, we invited work into our homes in a more invasive way than it had been in the past. Work responsibilities consumed day, night, and weekends due in some part to the nature of remote work but also because there were few activities to engage in outside of the home. Our children's sporting events and all social outings were wiped from our calendars, and we stayed at home. With little to do but binge-watch television and movies, we worked online through the evenings and weekends.

Our boundaries between work and home were blurred. When we finally physically returned to the office, some of the same habits of bringing work home continued. Leaders struggled to establish boundaries and delegate, which are both essential to being able to prioritize tasks. The time spent working or thinking about work suddenly increased exponentially.

Time is one of a leader's most valuable nonrenewable resources. The pressures of an overscheduled day leaves little room for creativity, brainstorming, and deep thinking. Leaders are often driven by a calendar of meetings and responsibilities. It can feel like a digital calendar on a mobile device drives every minute as the day melts away through back-to-back meetings. Electronic calendars resemble color-coded puzzles of obligations. Leaders fall prey to multitasking when trying to squeeze more tasks into the day.

The power of a pause—a vacation, even a long weekend—can rejuvenate and help refresh. Smaller pauses can also reinvigorate and reenergize when put to good use. A pause, even if brief, provides time to reflect and gain a new perspective, read professional books, or listen to a podcast. This provides the leader space to be reflective, creative, and strategic—a must when dealing with tasks that require high cognitive demand.

While the idea of a pause or break is appealing, too often leaders do the opposite and fill their days with multitasking on several technology devices at the same time. Multitasking can deceptively feel like a productive and efficient use of time. Overscheduled and overcommitted leaders find themselves stressed and at risk of losing the ability to reflect and think creatively. When we pile tasks on top of one another, answer emails during a meeting, or complete compliance forms while on the phone with someone who is sharing a concern, we are distracted and disengaged. We sacrifice our full attention. We sacrifice the quiet moments necessary for engagement and creative brainstorming. We then lose the opportunity to innovate in the noise of constant distractions.

Some leaders claim to do their best work when under pressure, at the eleventh hour. However, procrastination and multitasking inhibit creative thinking.[1] Creative solutions can rise in quiet times or pauses away from distractions. Leaders must allow themselves the space to be reflective and strategic.

Empowered women listen to their intuition, their gut. They use their intuition to consider what is best for their organization and the individuals it serves. But in overscheduled times of heated debates and distraction, the noise can drown out our internal voices. We may not be able to hear our internal voice. We must take a step away to surround ourselves with quiet reflection. Whether listening to a favorite playlist, journaling, meditating, or exercising with light yoga, the moments of reflection allow us to hear our inner voice again.

When we overschedule and overcommit, we lose time for creative thought and cognitive planning. Educators are busy and try to make the most of every minute of the workday. In an attempt to regain control of time, leaders analyze their calendars and reorganize, reschedule, or cancel meetings. They cut one meeting short or arrive late to another and answer emails in the midst of both. Strategically stacking meetings and responsibilities makes time management daunting. Rather than managing time, leaders should shift to a management of the mind.[2] This creates a project-based schedule, rather than a task-based schedule.

Not only are the minutes and hours of her own days nonrenewable but also those of her team. Adults who are required to attend meetings that feel like a waste of time become agitated and easily distracted. Leaders feel this way, but those we lead do as well. They want to feel their time is used efficiently and they are able to contribute to a discussion or brainstorm.

Leaders have the responsibility to start and end meetings on time. It is also important to display respect for others' time by creating an agenda prior to the meeting containing only items that require discussion. If an agenda item is a matter that can be communicated via email, it should not be on the meeting agenda. The leader should also facilitate nimble and efficient movement through the meeting.

Respect time as a nonrenewable resource for employees. Those we lead have limited attention spans due to busy lives and the constant pressure to multitask. Do not fill meetings with information you could easily share in an email. Keep emails and newsletters concise. Seek ways to reduce workload. Prepare an agenda for meetings, keep it concise, and stick to the predetermined start and end times. When it's time to wrap up, simply state, "I want to be respectful of your time . . ." and then close with a concise note of gratitude or schedule a follow-up meeting.

Because some meetings do not allow all participants to be heard or participants may not feel comfortable interjecting during the meeting, protocols should include an "around the room" opportunity at the end of a meeting. Each participant then has the opportunity to share any additional thoughts or ask questions. This end-of-meeting protocol allows each member to know they will always have the opportunity to contribute, even those who are reserved or unsure of their voice. A member who isn't as comfortable speaking during the meeting, such as a new team member, will have an opportunity to seek clarification at the end.

THE PERSPECTIVE OF TIME

Within a busy day, there can be a bad hour, but it does not mean the bad hour should translate to a bad day. Leaders who use the perspective of time to see the good are those who can persist through challenges and adversity.

When asked "How was your day?" it is a natural response to generalize and sigh, saying, "Ugh. Not so great." But if we allow ourselves to dig deeper, sometimes upon reflection, a bad day is not actually a bad day. It is a rough hour or a challenging thirty minutes. Perhaps an exchange with a colleague felt passive-aggressive during a thirty-minute meeting. Or perhaps a deadline was looming in the morning and made for extra work and stress for the team.

More often than not, when we think we had a bad day, it was actually that we only had a bad hour within the entire span of the day. We can have a bad hour or two but not a bad day. Leaders should be cautious when labeling the entire day as bad when perhaps there were only a few difficult hours of the day and the rest was OK or even very good. Simply reflecting on and renaming and then celebrating the good portions of the day is a step a leader can take to refocus.

The hours on a watch can help bring perspective because at the end of the day, you can have a bad hour and still have a good day. Similar to the ways our students are taught in a behavior modification program to record data on which hours of the day were good or bad, we too must give ourselves the grace to recognize we can have a few minutes or hours of the day that do not go the way we want them to but that those moments do not make the entire day a bad day. During challenging times, it can help to utter two simple sentences a few times, "I am having a bad moment in my day, but it is not going to last forever."

LEADERSHIP TIPS

- Be present in the moment.
- Ask yourself what your calendar reveals about your priorities. What does it reveal about your potential as a leader?
- Honor your time and others' time.
- Before a meeting, set an agenda with start and end times. Keep items concise. Does it require discussion or only the dissemination of information? If it can be emailed, it shouldn't be on the agenda.
- Put a bad moment in perspective. A bad hour is not a bad day.

Chapter 6

Mountaintop Moments

Women in leadership say they fear "Not knowing enough or being as accomplished as my peers."

In a society intoxicated by enviable social media posts and filtered snapshot pictures, it is easy to fall prey to comparisons to another person's life, physical attributes, possessions, or accomplishments. It is difficult to escape comparisons when we are inundated daily with top-of-the-mountain moments.

Mountaintop moments are those in which a huge achievement is celebrated. They are the moments that represent the pinnacle of success and achievement such as the completion of an advanced graduate degree or the final steps of a marathon. Mountaintop moments are the priceless moments individuals are proud to share with others to celebrate and announce their achievements. Pictures posted on social media show the very best of accomplishments.

Naturally, social media is used to spread good news of accomplishments because it is an efficient way to share personal news with friends and family. Announcements and congratulatory replies no longer have to wait for a card in the mail. In a few minutes after a social media post is made, hundreds of friends and family become part of the celebration and are able to interact with laudatory comments. While mountaintop moments should be shared and celebrated, there is danger in using them to compare ourselves to the achievements of a friend, family member, or colleague. When we see them as comparisons of achievement, the snapshots can evoke feelings of envy and jealousy, which then thwart our own success.

KENDRA'S LEADERSHIP STORY

In the final stages of writing her dissertation, Kendra felt an overwhelming sense of pressure. Piles of research articles and books lined the walls of her

43

home office, and her laptop was her constant companion. Her evenings and weekends were spent highlighting and citing research, and she rarely took a break for herself.

When she allowed herself a moment to peek at social media, Kendra would sometimes encounter feelings of deflation. The social media break actually made her feel worse because friends or colleagues would post a picture of their personal achievements after successfully defending and proudly proclaiming their new Dr. titles.

While Kendra was very happy for her friends, the feeling was overshadowed by Kendra's envy. She felt disappointed in herself because she had not yet completed her own journey. She spent many years writing and researching, and the end of the journey felt distant. Kendra was defeated to see their achievements. She wanted to be able to celebrate their achievements, but her frustration with herself stood in the way because she wished she too had accomplished the lofty goal.

In the posts, Kendra only saw their moment on the top of the mountain as they donned a graduation gown or posed for a selfie in front of a presentation slide with a dissertation title displayed. Those images did not open a window to their daily struggles with piles of research similar to hers. Like Kendra, they spent years prior to the mountaintop moment feeling stressed and pouring over research data. None of it was captured in pictures or posted on social media. The moments of climbing to the top of the mountain were not glamorous or exciting, so the moments shared on social media were only those on the top of the mountain. Pictures from a doctoral hooding ceremony do not show the boring hours sitting in front of a laptop, reading research, and highlighting many articles only to grab one sentence to cite.

Also similar to Kendra, the well-deserving new PhDs or EdDs had worked for years on their achievement. They were finished, but they too had many struggles along the way. She only saw their moments on the mountaintop, and it provoked envy in her, of which she felt ashamed. She publicly praised and congratulated them, but privately battled feelings of envy and frustration with her own slow progress up the mountain.

Kendra did not post pictures of herself reading research in a quiet office because she wouldn't have thought anyone wanted to glimpse into those moments. It was the unenviable and unenjoyable portion of the process. It never crossed her mind to post any part of her journey on social media except the moment she was hooded by her favorite professor and committee chair. Not pictured were challenging private moments where she would receive feedback and break down in tears, ready to give up, and then pick herself back up and start again.

LEARNING FROM KENDRA'S LEADERSHIP STORY

Pictures on the mountaintop are polished and beautiful, likely with filters or poses. Posts of a diploma and graduation robe or a new business card after a promotion are fun to share and celebrate. They are beautiful and worthy of celebration. But there are always moments of struggle and defeat in the journey to the mountaintop. Social media shows the top of the mountain moments, the proud moments of accomplishment. It rarely shows defeat. Viewing only the mountaintop moments of friends and colleagues can plague our own self-confidence.

Vince Lombardi said, "The man at the top of the mountaintop did not fall there." Moments at the top of the mountain are always preceded by challenges and struggles. The top of the mountain is posted, but the strenuous climb to the summit is not. While it may not be visible to others, the ascent is actually what makes the accomplishment so beautiful. The final moments on the mountaintop are magical primarily because of the effort it took to arrive. Untold stories in the professional ascent are lined with courage and strength.

I am not suggesting we should no longer post our celebratory mountaintop achievements. We should compliment each other on achievements and help one another celebrate, but we must also recognize the effort it took to arrive. When we fail to see the effort it took someone else to climb, we risk defeat ourselves. When we only see the peak of the mountain, we incorrectly presume it must have been easy to reach the mountaintop moment. When our own ascent is not as easy, we give up or abandon our own dream. Focusing only on the peak of achievement, thereby, jeopardizes the desire to journey toward the goal.

We should never use the mountaintop moments of others as a comparison to our own worth or success. They should not be a tool of self-destruction based on the fact that we haven't yet reached the summit of the mountain ourselves. We each have our different points at which we are on the mountain. That does not make our journey any less valuable or important. But if you're not in a space to be able to see others at their peak, avoid viewing social media until you are. Then join in their celebration and allow others to help celebrate your mountaintop moments.

CELEBRATIONS

It is not only achievements that should be celebrated and lauded. The effort and work to arrive should as well. Celebrate achievements but also the climb.

We must be willing to congratulate ourselves for mountaintop moments but also for the mid-mountaintop moments.

Along the way to the mountaintop moment, small achievements should also be celebrated. How powerful could it be if we replace our *To Do lists* with *Celebrations lists*? We could regularly make lists of the small-scale and the significant accomplishments or the positive moments in our lives. We could use them to inspire our next step to the top of the mountain while we shout praise for the mountaintop moments of others.

Recall a moment you felt weak or challenged and out of place, a moment when you were climbing the mountain toward success but felt incapable of reaching the top of the mountain. Recall the details of what was happening. Return to the specific moment and re-create it with a power statement and presence.

Next, consider a moment you felt strong and powerful, with energy that could light up a room. Use that feeling to fashion a power mantra of self-affirming positive statements. Then, turn them into a routine of self-support and encouragement. Rehearse a statement until it is stuck in your mind, like a song stuck in your head. Then, go to the power mantra when you have moments of doubt.

Perhaps the following can be your power mantra: "Sweet Girl, you are on your way to the mountaintop. When you arrive, arrive humbly. Shout praise for your mountaintop moment, but don't forget the challenges you overcame to accomplish your goals."

When you write your power mantra, you reframe your internal voice. This is important because the one person's voice you listen to the most often is your own. And most often the voice is talking about you. Tell her what you would tell a friend, a respected colleague, someone you are mentoring.

It is dangerous to watch another woman's mountaintop moments assuming it was easy for her, assuming she never felt defeated along the way and never felt vulnerable. The more confident and assured the other woman appears, the more frustrated we might feel if it is not equally as easy for us. However, it truly was not easy for her either. She met challenges along the way to her success as well. Even if her challenges were private, she, too, struggled and overcame obstacles on her climb to the top of the mountain.

Pictures on the mountaintop are polished and beautiful, like a face covered in makeup, shadow, and lipstick. They are beautiful and worthy of celebration. However, we are lying to ourselves when we do not recognize the natural beauty of a face without makeup or an ascent to the top of the mountain. We cannot let the makeup of others hurt our personal self-esteem or self-worth. Similar to makeup, social media and videoconferencing programs use filters to make us look well rested, younger, even thinner. But they are not real. Reality requires hard work, effort, defeat, and challenges. If we forget to embrace those moments as well as the beautiful moments, we risk giving up when challenges arise.

LEADERSHIP TIPS

- Moments on the top of the mountain are preceded by unenviable struggles and effort.
- Allow yourself grace, knowing the struggles are part of the journey to the top of the mountain.
- Don't ruminate on other's mountaintop moments. Rather, choose to embrace your climb as a journey and celebrate small achievements along the way.

Chapter 7

Self-Reflection and Accountability

Women in leadership say they fear "Losing sight of my 'why,' the legacy I want to leave."

Successful leaders have a high level of self-awareness. They regularly check in on their own strengths, weaknesses, opportunities, and threats (otherwise referred to as SWOT), much like an organization might do. A SWOT analysis assists an organization in establishing goals by offering a visual representation of areas of celebration and challenge. It can also be an effective self-reflection tool to help the leader dig deeper into her own needs.

She can ask herself, "What are my strengths and weaknesses? What are my opportunities for growth and future achievement? What might threaten those opportunities?" After creating a list for each prompt, she can use the analysis to determine what she wishes to accomplish and how she might achieve it. She can also use brainstorming to disarm the issues that threaten her success.

REBECCA'S LEADERSHIP STORY

Rebecca knew she wanted to lead a school district when she became a principal. She watched her mentor, a graceful superintendent who was nearing retirement, lead the district with heart. Her mentor treated others the way she personally wanted to be treated and approached situations with empathy and compassion. She worked hard to see another person's perspective, even when the other person was an angry parent on the other end of a phone call.

Five years into her role as the principal, Rebecca was given the opportunity to lead a nearby school district in which her own young children attended. The district posted a vacancy, and she pounced at the chance to lead. Rebecca had ideas and hopes and dreams for the district and felt she knew what it needed because she watched the district from her parent lens for several years. On her first days in her new office, Rebecca made lists of the items she planned to address. Some of them would require her immediate attention, while others could wait a few months, she told herself.

Rebecca felt fortunate to have seven board members who supported her and wanted to see her succeed. But everything changed on election night after her first year in the position. One April evening, she knew things were changing when three new board members were elected, one who had been vocally aggressive and demanding during public comment of previous board meetings. The board who hired Rebecca unanimously showed her their support. She knew that would all change now.

The days and weeks following the board elections were riddled with multiple emails from Vicky, a new board member who had aggressively stated her doubts in Rebecca's leadership. Some days Vicky would send Rebecca ten emails. Some asked for reports and information; other emails were attacks on Rebecca's competence.

From one day to the next, Vicky's push and pull changed. She would question the number of times Rebecca called the district's attorney. Vicky would ask why she had to call legal counsel when the district paid Rebecca a high enough salary that she should know the answers herself. The very next day, Vicky would ask Rebecca why she hadn't contacted the attorney, as there was vital information the board needed to have and they deserved to know what the attorney recommended.

Vicky's barrage of emails and constant doubt mentally and physically drained Rebecca. She wanted to prove to Vicky she was capable and resourceful. She found herself spending a large amount of time responding to this one board member and trying to appease her. After weeks of stress, Rebecca questioned whether she was in the right field and whether she should look for another job or another career.

Rebecca allowed Vicky's voice to plant doubt in her own mind, and she spent most of her days trying to address Vicky's concerns. Vicky expected her to justify and defend every decision she made. Rebecca's attention to Vicky's unreasonable demands left little time for her to address concerns from other board members or staff. She had allowed Vicky to dominate her attention at the expense of more critical priorities.

Rebecca realized her priorities were misaligned when one of her other seven board members suggested she had not been communicating with them enough. She recognized she was communicating often with Vicky, but the rest of the board was not aware. They felt out of communication and began to question Rebecca's transparency.

Rebecca decided to take a step back from the situation and self-reflect. She made a list of her strengths, weaknesses, opportunities, and threats. She realized the biggest threat to her time was the energy she spent on Vicky's independent concerns and requests. Rebecca reached out to her board president and shared how often Vicky called or emailed and demanded information and responses. She printed the many emails she received every day. Rebecca illustrated how it was not only draining on her as the leader but also consuming her time. Rebecca explained to the board president that she felt obligated to respond to Vicky's many requests because Vicky was one of her seven direct supervisors. Rebecca wanted to navigate the threat in a professional manner and needed her board president's support and guidance.

The board president also recognized the situation with Vicky was out of control and met with her to discuss it. He told Vicky requests of the superintendent's time would need to come from the majority of the board. He provided examples of the way seven separate voices pulling on Rebecca's time and attention would cause chaos and deter from the work that needed to be completed. He reminded her that her legal authority was during a publicly convened meeting when her fellow board members were present. He asked that Vicky make any requests in a meeting so all board members could weigh in on whether Rebecca or her team should spend the time necessary to complete them.

The board president was able to address Vicky's actions, but Rebecca continued to doubt herself and her ability to lead. She had allowed Vicky's doubt to become her internal voice. She allowed her ambition and confidence to be rocked by Vicky's negativity. Rebecca had a choice. She could allow Vicky to pull her down and potentially steer her into a less demanding career, or she could reset her personal goals and priorities.

Rebecca chose to take control. She went back to her personal SWOT analysis and reminded herself she had many strengths and opportunities. She allowed her board president to navigate the issues with Vicky, and she self-reflected on her priorities. After several months of intentional work on her SWOT analysis, Rebecca felt more balanced and centered. As author Lalah Delia said, "She remembered who she was and the game changed."

LEARNING FROM REBECCA'S LEADERSHIP STORY

Personal goals pave the way to success. But without self-reflection and discipline, goals are only hopes. When Rebecca outlined her strengths, weaknesses, opportunities, and threats, she was able to begin her personal growth story. She was able to address the biggest threat to her success at the time, her demanding board member. But the self-reflection continued. As the next step in the process, she asked herself, "What activities fill my day? What professional books am I reading? Do they align to my goals? If not, what changes am I willing to make?"

She wondered, "How do I see myself? How do others see me? Are the two aligned?" This deeper reflection not only explored what those around her expected to see but who Rebecca was at her core.

Leaders often focus on how others see them. We must hold up the mirror and self-reflect, not based on the standards others expect, but based on our standards for ourselves. A pause to look in the rearview mirror helps leaders learn and grow from experiences and mistakes, but perhaps more critical than reflection is the difficult task of looking in the mirror to self-reflect. Both are necessary for a productive and fulfilling life.

Successful leaders are able to self-reflect, adjust, and improve. They use self-analysis for personal growth but not in a self-destructive way. They use it as a best friend would, to offer constructive feedback and support, to propel them forward. This is possible if priorities are aligned to values. Would you talk to a friend or colleague the way you talk to yourself? Even during challenging times, there are things of which to be proud and to celebrate.

Female leaders ruminate over negative feedback from one individual even when they hear praise from many other people at the same time. They allow the one negative voice to fester internally.[1] Women search for affirmation and praise.[2] Women internalize their frustrations and are not as apt to communicate them with others, because they want to please.

One tip to counter this self-destructive pattern is to maintain a "feel good file" in which letters, cards, and emails can be stored for years. Any positive letter or email you receive should be placed in the file. Then, when situations shake your confidence, take a dive into the file to reread a few at a time. Remind yourself of the positive influence you've had over others and their gratitude for you.

PROFESSIONAL GOALS

Setting goals can look similar to the learning process. When children are taught to comprehend narrative text, their instruction is explicit. Throughout the process of reading a story, teachers model the importance of making predictions based on the text. Students then learn to monitor the prediction as they continue to read the rest of the story and learn more about the characters or plot. As the narrative progresses, near the end, students are encouraged to adjust the prediction, abandon it, or confirm it. Similar to this process, a leader's goals should be established, monitored, and adjusted. And on occasion, goals may need to be abandoned, much like predictions are abandoned when reading a good book.

Goal setting should begin by defining success but also defining joy. Success and joy are personal and unique to each leader. Individuals define them in different ways. When self-reflection accompanies goal setting, steps to improvement can be clearly outlined, monitored, and achieved.

As an example, one of Rebecca's professional goals was to empower female leaders through the creation of a strong network and professional learning. On the surface, to hear women's stories of perseverance was something that made her feel good and reenergized her. But when she heard their stories, she was reminded of the attacks Vicky launched against her solely because she was a woman in a historically male-dominated career. The stories from her colleagues brought back the emotions of vulnerability she thought she had overcome.

Rebecca's board member, Vicky, was often angry and would point her finger in Rebecca's face, scream at her, and doubt anything she said. She left professional scars on Rebecca's confidence. At the time it was happening, Rebecca hesitated to share her struggles with anyone because she felt very vulnerable. She worried about the damage Vicky could do to her career, even though the defaming comments were untrue. Rebecca did not reach out to her network because she worried she might appear weak.

Rebecca's motivation for her professional goal of building a strong support system for women centered around the fact that she knew there were women struggling in situations similar to what she was able to overcome. She wanted them to know they were not alone and did not need to endure the unjust treatment in isolation.

In times of distress such as Rebecca endured, it is critical to find a quiet moment to reflect. Ask yourself: What do you want? What is your dream? Who is this for? How do you define success, joy? What inspires YOU?

The following reflection questions can further guide your self-reflection:

Professional Aspiration/Mountaintop Moment?
Why do I want to achieve this?
Motivation/Reward?
Date to begin?
Frequency of little step celebrations?
Date of culminating celebration?
Necessary resources?
Obstacles to overcome?
Little steps?
Big steps?
What am I willing to give up/forgo in order to achieve the above? Will this
    be a temporary or permanent sacrifice?

Once goals are established and a commitment is made to achieve them, they should be turned into healthy daily rituals or routines. Routines must be habitual to be effective. They must become a part of every day, as positive intentions for success. And finally, celebrations and rewards must be built in for each step toward the final goal.

LEADERSHIP TIPS

- Talk to yourself the way you would talk to a friend or colleague.
- Never accept criticism from individuals you wouldn't go to for advice.
- Reset your priorities when you find yourself floundering.

Chapter 8

Communication

Women in leadership say they fear "Being misunderstood."

Skilled leaders possess strong communication skills and make efforts to continue to hone them. They value the ability to effectively communicate—to be clearly understood and to understand. Strong leaders use empathy and understanding of another's perspective to guide the information they share and the manner in which they communicate. They ask, "What would parents want to know about this situation?" or "How would staff best be able to understand this message?"

Conversely when leaders neglect to communicate in a strategic manner, staff, parents, or community members fill in the blanks on their own, with pieces of information. In the absence of communication from a leader, misinformation abounds. Individuals are left to guess and assume. Effective and timely communication should be one of a leader's top priorities.

KRYSTAL'S LEADERSHIP STORY

Krystal's school district watched their student enrollment increase steadily for two decades. Their community was a suburb of a nearby large urban city, and families were drawn to the hometown feel it provided. Residential construction boomed, and students filled classrooms. The schools used every available space for classrooms as their enrollment grew year after year. The trajectory meant the district would soon need to add on to the schools or construct a new school building.

Prior to initiating a campaign to pass a tax referendum, Krystal recognized the need to communicate clearly and honestly with her community. As the superintendent of a school district that served as the heart of her community, Krystal felt a duty to ensure its success, but she also knew the topic of a tax increase would have many outspoken opponents in the community. Krystal predicted the enrollment growth in her community meant the school district would need to add a new elementary school within the next handful of years. Backing into the date of the end goal of a new construction, she knew two years would be required for design and build, two years for passing a referendum and selling of bonds, and one year for preparation of the referendum information. Krystal and her team needed to act quickly.

The first steps in the five-year planning process were critical. State law required voters to approve both the request to sell bonds and the request to construct a new school. Krystal worked closely with her board of education and administrative cabinet to identify the need and articulate it to taxpayers. Many brochures, social media posts, and newsletter articles were drafted to explain the need for the project and the downfalls of a possible rejection.

Despite the hours and hours she spent creating flyers and drafting newsletter articles, Krystal heard parents were buzzing with misinformation. There was a small community group spreading untrue bullet points about the tax rate increase. Krystal knew she needed to combat the gossip and misleading statements.

Krystal and her leadership team identified several parents who were supportive and several who were known to be vocally opposed to district initiatives but tended to be open-minded individuals. She asked them to become a committee of stakeholders she called Key Communicators. Krystal's vision for the Key Communicators was to gain their insight about concerns in the community. In turn she could share detailed information with them they could then share with friends and community members. The Key Communicators would be the first to receive information from the district, including details of the referendum campaign. They would be able to review her articles on various topics before anyone else and could provide feedback or ask her to include other details.

Krystal and the ten Key Communicators met every two weeks for an hour. Their informal discussions were kept in confidence. They agreed to provide insight before information was released. When she asked what they felt parents and taxpayers would want to know, Krystal heard over and over again how communication needed to be concise if she wanted to ensure it would be read.

They all agreed parents were busy and inundated with information from the schools and teachers. Busy working parents didn't have time to read long email blasts. This insight was eye-opening for Krystal because while the topics were top priorities for her, it was helpful to understand the perspective of a busy parent who only had a few minutes to digest information from the district office.

Krystal revamped her approach to communicating. She replaced long newsletter articles with graphics and bulleted lists of concise, easily ingested information. Parents and community members responded positively to her new approach. One told Krystal that she reads school emails while parked in her car waiting for her children to be dismissed from school. She only had three to five minutes to learn all she could about district news, so she appreciated the more concise approach.

The Key Communicators functioned as first-level communicators, offering and receiving information before Krystal shared it with the broader community. They often brought Krystal helpful information they heard from local taxpayers who did not have children in the schools. They emphasized the importance of seeing a situation from various perspectives before communicating.

One Key Communicator shared the story of a retired couple in the district who were surprisingly very supportive of the tax referendum. She said she respected their position because they noted the value of the schools for those who no longer have children who use the schools. Their children were grown, and grandchildren lived in other states. However, the couple said the strength of the schools directly correlated to their property value. They knew that when it was time to sell their home, the strength of the schools would determine their resale value more than the number of bedrooms they could offer or the age of their kitchen cabinets. Krystal shared this story with the television news media who asked her to comment on the referendum. She focused on this story and a few additional key points she wanted the media to hear because she knew they would also interview opponents to the campaign.

As she reflected on the need to be concise with communication, Krystal also recognized her need to manage messages efficiently, for her own productivity and sanity. Her days were often filled answering questions, often the same questions asked by multiple parents or staff. She felt obligated to reply quickly to their questions or concerns. Krystal cut and pasted replies, but found even copying text to be an overwhelming task because she received emails daily. She pushed out emails as quickly as possible and spent a lot of time to ensure each received a reply.

Krystal turned to a technology solution. She created an FAQ page on a Google Doc of which only she had editing rights. As parents would email her with commonly asked questions, Krystal would list the question and answer on the doc. Then she would reply to the parent simply thanking them for the email and directing them to the FAQ for the reply. The FAQ could be updated frequently, but it allowed Krystal to streamline communication and provide a central location for information sharing. Rather than expecting parents or staff to dig through newsletters or social media posts for information, they were able to find it easily.

Krystal's improvements in the area of communication not only helped the district pass the tax referendum, but it also helped her be an even more successful superintendent. She continued to meet with the Key Communicators once a quarter and continued to improve her style of communication. Krystal felt her relationships with them were mutually beneficial and rewarding, so much so that she encouraged them to consider someday running for a position on the school board.

LEARNING FROM KRYSTAL'S LEADERSHIP STORY

Through her work with the Key Communicators, Krystal increased her tools for communication. Strong leadership requires effective communication. The most successful leaders have strong communication skills and understand how much and in what way to best communicate. Leaders communicate for the following reasons:

- To *share information*, such as data, facts, guidance, news, instructions, vision
- To *build relationships* and establish trust
- To *seek input* and gain insight/new points of view or see new perspectives
- To *inspire action* from others and mobilize them to act or negotiate an outcome

SHARING INFORMATION

Skilled leaders share information in a concise and timely manner. Krystal honed her communication skills when she realized parents were receiving an overwhelming amount of information that they did not have the bandwidth to consume. She learned to use written communication that was easy to read and understand because correspondence with too much detail comes across as noisy and distracting to a reader.

Rather than providing too many details, Krystal revised her messages to include references to additional resources or links to more information. Ironically, writing concisely actually took more effort, though fewer words were written, because Krystal spent the time to pare down messages to only include the most important information. But Krystal knew the information was more likely to be read when it was succinct so the extra time to condense was worthwhile.

Leaders trained in communication skills view themselves as headliners. They communicate concisely to ensure the message is read or heard. Salient points are emphasized, and ancillary information is left out or added to an addendum for those who want more detail. This allows the attention to be given to the most important parts of the message. Messages that include overly descriptive, repeated information are more likely to be ignored or skimmed.

The ability to communicate clearly and concisely is a skill that must be developed. Women tend to provide many details, especially in oral communication. To clarify a point, they restate a few different ways until others nod in understanding or agreement. This may be genetically inherent, or perhaps it comes from a nurturing standpoint based on our childhood days of "playing school" when we restated thoughts to ensure they were understood. While there is no harm in ensuring the message is understood and received, restating the same idea multiple ways can result in its being ignored or the leader's coming across that she is unsure of herself.

Women in leadership must, therefore, make an intentional effort to keep written and spoken communication succinct when possible. When drafting communication, it is best to proactively anticipate the questions the reader might ask and clearly address them so the message is not ambiguous. It is also helpful to have someone else read the message before it is sent, to ensure it is clear and easily understood.

Spoken communication should also be concise but needs to come across genuinely with eye contact and active listening. If a female leader is eager to please and wants to ensure her point is understood, she can tend to restate or repeat. Without realizing it, she may circle back to the same topic repetitively during a conversation to ensure she is understood. This cycle tends to repeat until the listener acknowledges confirmation or understanding.

Messages are also conveyed through the use of body language. While what you say and how you say it are important, the way you look when you say it is even more significant, and often overlooked. The words we use to communicate messages matter, but the way in which we say them can negate or confirm the message. Subtle gestures or facial expressions can send an opposite message of the words directly stated. A confident leader will make a plan that outlines what she will say, how she will say it, and how she wants to look when she says it. For example, if she is sitting, she will ensure her hands are above the table. If she is telling her team she appreciates them, she will not shift her eyes to her phone.

When the leader is delivering a formal communication such as a speech or presentation, she should stand confidently and use strategically placed pauses to encourage listeners to reflect on the message. There is a great deal of power in the quiet moments of a presentation or conversation. The pause or moment of silence provides the opportunity for listeners to reflect more deeply.

Leaders are faced with many scenarios in which they will need to deliver information that is difficult to receive. Communication of difficult matters requires honesty, empathy, and transparency to the extent as professionally possible. Leaders should be objective and concise and communicate with reserved emotion.

Leaders who can remain calm and poised, especially in challenging situations, are determined and gritty. The ability to maintain poise and kindness in stressful situations is resilience and stoicism. It is the sign of power and self-control.

Leaders are in a position to share information on a wider basis than most, through media interviews and articles. Some of the most talented leaders struggle with television news interviews because interviewing is a skill that must be practiced. Too often leaders don't take the time to rehearse interviewing skills, and then a heated issue arises that they must address on camera. The bright light from a video camera shines in their face and they freeze.

Communication with the media requires rehearsal and a script. A wise leader practices her interview with a colleague or staff member prior to the interview. The second the bright light from a journalist's news camera is turned on is the moment all ability to critically analyze the situation is diminished. If unrehearsed or not used to this scenario, a leader will often flounder and stumble over words.

A leader should remember she has the ability to drive the interview. Especially when she is the sole interviewee on a topic, it is hers to control and navigate. She has the power to take the reins. If she wishes to pause the interview, she should feel comfortable requesting a brief recess.

To sound articulate, begin with a bulleted list of important talking points. Never veer from the list when responding to reporters. Stick to the script, even if it seems like you're not answering the questions the reporter poses. When the interview topic is controversial or heated, it is the reporter's job to pull a leader's direction away from the script and try to catch a salacious comment that could later be used to cultivate controversy and garner an audience.

Media journalists are friendly, but it is not their job to be your friend, nor should you view them as such. You need to be on guard but kind and professional. Their job is to make sure the story receives attention and social media likes and clicks. And finally, leaders should assume what they say in an interview, write in an email, or post online will be widely distributed via social media copy/paste and reposts.[1]

BUILDING RELATIONSHIPS

Leaders who hear concerns and complaints and handle confrontational conversations with empathy are filled with strength. A compassionate, empathetic leader listens and guides. She interjects when necessary but wants to glean information from those in her presence. But compassion and active listening should not be viewed as weakness or fragility. Rather, it takes considerable strength to be a compassionate leader.

The leader mustn't always be the smartest person in the room. There is no need to pretend to be. Compassionate leaders do not enter conversations with the goal of self-promotion. They avoid the tendency to insert "one-up" stories. One-up stories occur when individuals fall prey to trying to impress or prove themselves by relating a similar experience they've had. While the intent may be to relate to a story, often those one-up stories are perceived as placing the priority back on the listener, rather than building a rapport from a similar experience. The listener may have a similar story but may not have experienced it the same way. Compassionate leaders know when it is appropriate to share a story to point out a similarity and when it is better to simply listen to understand.

A strong leader is selective in what she says. She is comfortable with quietly reflecting as others speak. She waits to speak until she has information to share that is crucial or helpful. She can comfortably be the person in the room who sits quietly because when she speaks, she does so with purpose, as a reflective leader.

Being a reflective leader also means being honest and transparent when something doesn't go right. Honest and transparent communication requires a leader to concede to wrongdoing if necessary. Genuine apologies strengthen relationships and build trust. When you mess up, fess up. Everyone, even the most skilled leader, has opportunities in which a mistake is made, or the leader could improve. Leaders can make the mistake of fearing honesty and transparency when they are wrong, assuming the admission of guilt is going to make them appear weak. However, it can actually do the inverse and build trust levels if a leader shares with the team how she made a mistake.

It is a leader's responsibility to take the steps to build and nurture relationships in order to establish trust. When the leader takes action that results in issues, she can rebuild trust if she is honest and tells the team she would like an opportunity to do better. Recognition and acceptance are what they wish to hear from her. They want to know things will change and improve. Staff see through a leader's attempt to cover up or make excuses for errors. Rather, being honest and vulnerable helps build relationships, especially when the leader expresses confidence in her ability to address staff concerns.

If it is the employee who has erred, the leader must also enter the conversation with respect, specifically so that the employee's self-dignity may remain intact. Meetings with employees who have done something inappropriate or performed poorly can be challenging, especially for a leader who values relationships and wants to instill loyalty to the organization. An example might be when an employee is being disciplined or terminated for cause. The leader should plan specifically what she will say so that when the employee becomes upset or angry, the conversation remains orderly and professional. If a list of bulleted points to discuss and remedies are prepared before the meeting, the leader can use them to guide the conversation that may become heated.

The best way to approach the tough conversations is to begin by stating, "I have some concerns I need to address with you, is this a good time? Are you in a good position to listen objectively and professionally?" This opening allows the employee to share if the timing is not good. For example, if the employee recently lost a parent or is going through a divorce, the leader might not have been aware.

Sharing difficult information can be challenging, but leaders are most effective when they focus on the action of the employee while maintaining respect for the individual. Be tough on the issues, soft on the people.

SEEKING INPUT

Leaders communicate to gain insight or new perspectives from those they lead. Being the one in the room who is willing to listen, rather than feeling the need to always speak, signals respect for others and their perspectives. Furthermore, providing time for their input to resonate and be understood is also a sign of skilled restraint. Both are more powerful than talking over others only to hear yourself speak and to appear like the only one in the room with answers worthy of being heard.

Leaders serve well when they actively listen and wait for an opportunity to share their own thoughts, rather than talking over others with the "right" answer. While it may be more efficient to cut off an employee's thoughts and correct him, what matters most is how the employee is able to process his own thinking juxtaposed to the dialogue. Often, an individual who is allowed to share an idea will later abandon it, but saying it out loud allows them to work through a different viewpoint. When a group is brainstorming, not every statement must be the solution. Some are merely options to be considered and later abandoned. Allowing an individual to talk through ideas and not feel judged, rushed, or hushed is a critical part of brainstorming.

This type of active listening means approaching a conversation as if you have something you wish to learn. Rather than listening to respond, actively listening means listening to learn and understand. Active listening requires the leader to avoid the tendency to think of a reply or a way to refute the idea. Because leaders are accustomed to addressing questions or concerns quickly, this can be a challenge. The leader may tend to use the time someone else is speaking to think about their reply.

There is as much to be said in the silence as there is in the spoken words. Listening to respond is distracting and does not allow the leader to hear the emotions behind an individual's statement. The leader is unable to absorb what she is being told and the passion behind it. Rather, to actively listen, she must practice restating what was shared. It is also key to pause and reflect before replying.

Seeking input and listening require patience. Especially when emotions are heightened, what is not said can be more important than what is. Sometimes the moments of pause, the moments of silence in a discussion, are more valuable than what is said. A leader can acknowledge staff and respect their input by simply nodding, without trying to fix. She shows respect for their input by restating their concerns and pausing for their reflection.

Skilled leaders use active listening and empathy to de-escalate conflict but also to de-escalate frustration or concerns. When speaking to a concerned parent, you can show compassion by saying, "You are your child's biggest advocate, and I respect your perspective. I want to hear your concerns and look into it further."

When staff are willing to share their concerns, it is because they want to know something will change. The leader should stay positive and show them she is open to making changes and then do so by following through with any promises made.

In conflict the leader needs to model understanding. She should beware of sounding dismissive, even when in a hurry. This issue is important to this individual, evidenced by the time they took to call, email, or come to see you. Show compassion rather than judgment or arrogance.

This level of restraint can be challenging because the leader must stop trying to fix problems or find perfect solutions. Individuals must be provided an opportunity to verbally explore their ideas without feeling the leader has all of the answers. Sometimes they simply want to know they are being heard and that their input is respected. That level of respect does not require all ideas to be accepted, only that they be heard and respected.

If a concern is brought to the leader, she should promise to look into the matter. However, she must be careful not to make promises that cannot be kept. Respecting and listening to another person's concerns does not require agreement. When actively listening, the leader should turn her body toward the individual who is speaking and use a smile or nod to model understanding.

Leaders are often confronted with negative feedback. Sometimes it is delivered anonymously via social media outlets. Don't take complaints personally. Tell yourself, "This is not about me." Rather than debating a comment by attempting to refute it online, it is best to simply ask the person who posted to reach out to you directly to discuss the misunderstanding. This allows others who are watching the exchange see that you addressed it directly, but it keeps the drama out of the public light.

While a leader spends much of her time transmitting and relaying information in written form or verbally in meetings, communication is more than simply the words spoken or written by a leader. Informal meetings, dialogue, and phone calls are not always as efficient but can be a more effective way to communicate than formal newsletters, emails, or reports. Authentic communication requires a significant time commitment and a high level of empathy from the leader in order to be well received. Empathetic leaders who dedicate time to both formal, efficient communication channels and informal, face-to-face methods are able to make true connections and understand the needs of the organization.

INSPIRING ACTION

Leaders also need strong communication skills when inspiring employees to take action, for example, when providing performance evaluation feedback. Staff want feedback from their leader. When a leader ignores a staff member, the employee's chances of being unhappy and disengaged from the work are as high as 40 percent. If the leader's feedback focuses primarily on weaknesses, the likelihood of disengagement is 22 percent. However if the feedback is focused on the employee's strengths, the employee's chance of being unhappy or disengaged drops to a mere 1 percent.[2]

A leader can inspire employees to take action in the way she communicates constructive feedback in performance evaluations, informal conversations, or disciplinary meetings. The feedback can be tailored to the employee's strengths, even when it is constructive criticism. When communicating constructive feedback, a leader should be honest and concise and avoid inserting herself into the feedback. Remember, this is not about you. She should avoid phrases like "If it were me, I would have done . . ." or "I provided this employee information to improve . . ." Not only does the first-person language come across as informal; it also sends a selfish message. The feedback comes across as selfish and judgmental, rather than supportive and constructive.

Rather, feedback should be crystal clear regarding next steps for improvement, in bullets if possible, to draw attention to priorities. For example, "To make more efficient use of time, ..." or "Attention to . . . should be provided more focus."

Communicating to share information, build relationships, seek input, or inspire individuals to take action is a leader's responsibility. She is most effective when she approaches with empathy or understanding for the other person's perspective and needs.

LEADERSHIP TIPS

- Be concise and to the point. Before sending a message, review and condense it.
- Actively listen to understand. Speak fewer words for a bigger impact.
- Don't solely seek input from those who will agree with you. Engage neutrals and nay-sayers in first-level communication on challenging topics.

Chapter 9

Building Consensus and Respect

Women in leadership say they fear "Not being respected" and "Not being able to lead the organization through conflict."

Every dynamic organization has moments in which conflict between members must be managed. But conflict must not be ignored. Left untended, conflict breeds disagreements, and disagreements can be interpreted as personal attacks. Rather than allowing conflict to become personal and long-lasting, a strong leader will spend the necessary time to help individuals build consensus.

The leader must first be able to garner respect before she can guide the organization through conflict or disagreement. She leads by example by being tough on issues but soft on people and tender with relationships. In this way, she earns respect from those she leads because she is able to pull a team together as their leader while not ignoring the issues. She is viewed as the captain of the ship in turbulent waters.

SIERRA'S LEADERSHIP STORY

Sierra's school district employed over three hundred elementary, middle school, and high school teachers. Each teacher was in different seasons of their careers and each had different perspectives and priorities, especially when it came to their compensation and benefits and employment contract provisions. A few months before the union and board teams began contract negotiations, Sierra proposed to her union leadership the idea of using an interest-based bargaining (IBB) style to negotiate the contract renewal. She heard about it from a colleague and saw it as a way to maintain good relationships between management and the employee group.

The board's negotiation team and the union's negotiation team agreed to attend IBB training together in advance of their first negotiations meeting. The twenty-two leaders spent a weekend learning how to identify and articulate interests and goals with mock scenarios. The trainer explained everyone would need to remove their work title "hats" and see themselves as an equal member of a large group that would brainstorm solutions and ideas based on pre-identified interests.

The training taught the members to identify mutual interests as a common ground through the use of fictitious practice scenarios such as negotiating the sale of a used car. They rehearsed the steps to negotiating by beginning with their common interests. In small groups, they saw how collegial the process could be if they learned to understand and respect one another's interests prior to digging into details of the negotiations. At the end of the IBB training scenarios, all twenty-two leaders felt energized and positive about the upcoming negotiations meetings. Participants had new tools for active listening and collaboration and also had established stronger relationships with one another.

Sierra knew the group would still face challenges in negotiations but appreciated the ability for all to start on a level footing and equally prepared for negotiations. She and the board had developed seven interest areas to bring to the first meeting, including the interest in attracting and retaining quality educators. Sierra was pleased when the union's six interest areas were very similar to the board's. It was clear both wanted the district to be the best it could.

Meetings that followed always started with a review of the group's norm agreements and the areas of interest the group would use for the focus of the meeting. Because a solid working relationship was developed during the mock activities of the IBB training, all members felt comfortable sitting intermingled in the meetings rather than sitting on opposite sides of the room. The group enjoyed each other's company and had plenty of small talk and laughter as meetings began and ended.

A month into the negotiations meetings when topics of salary and benefits arose, interactions changed. Small talk and laughter transformed into reserved and formal responses. The teams tackled tough conversations about the district's finances and increases to health insurance benefits. The employee union leadership strongly believed the family health insurance plan needed to be more affordable and the district should cover more of the cost of the premiums. The board team felt it would be better able to recruit new teachers if those dollars were placed in base salaries. Both groups gave reasons for their perspective, and it felt like an agreement was far from reach.

Sierra felt the mood in the room shift. She feared the progress and goodwill earned to that point would quickly derail. She knew she needed to help the group reset and revisit the core tenets of the IBB training. Sierra facilitated a review of the articulated interests and visually lined them up on a large chart she hung on the wall. She asked each of the group members to point out what they saw as commonalities in their groups' interests. It was clear the two teams had lost sight of their common goal and needed to find a third option. The third option might not be exactly what either side wanted but each side could accept.

Because Sierra was willing to articulate and point out the struggle, the progress continued, and relationships remained professional and productive. As the leader, Sierra saw her role as one to remind members to revisit the group norms, the common agreements, and the need to actively listen to one another. Throughout the negotiation process, there were disagreements, but they were rooted in mutual agreement and respect. Trusted relationships were, therefore, not only sustained but also strengthened.

LEARNING FROM SIERRA'S LEADERSHIP STORY

Some of the most stressful times for school district leaders are the moments of disagreement and conflict. Specifically challenging can be disagreements between the board of education and the teacher's union when the two must negotiate wages and working conditions. Heated debates and differing opinions can tear apart relationships if the leader does not keep a calm and poised approach to consensus building.

Consensus is not synonymous with universal agreement. Not everyone must agree 100 percent for a group to reach consensus. Rather, consensus is reached when everyone feels comfortable with the outcome or decision and will commit to live with it. In a consensus, all members agree not to sabotage or undermine a final decision of the group.

Skilled leaders know the steps to build consensus and recognize the value in the process. Building consensus requires taking a step back, emotionally, which can be the first point of failure for many. If a leader takes the situation personally, she is not able to progress strategically. If she allows her emotions or the emotions of those within the group to guide the process, those she leads will do the same, and group dynamics will be negatively affected.

While every leader hopes to build consensus within meetings, hope is not a strategy. A leader must intentionally and proactively take steps to build consensus. After removing emotion from a meeting or specific situation, she next needs to help the groups identify a common goal. For example, during a contract negotiation, both the union and the management should identify their ultimate success goals. Likely, both would say they are interested in attracting and retaining high-quality employees. When both groups are willing to articulate and commit to a common goal, they begin on the same page and are poised to build consensus.

If it is difficult to identify a common goal, start small. Begin by articulating areas of agreement, for example, "We agree this topic is important to our organization." A simple beginning such as that can build rapport because each group member will begin to nod in acceptance that the topic is a priority. If it was not, they likely would not have agreed to attend the meeting, so this is a good starting point to agreement. It can be used as an initial step to naming a shared purpose and intention. From there, the leader should encourage the team to continue on until a common goal is identified.

Throughout the work, it is critical to revisit the common goal. Each time the groups meet, the common goal should be restated as a reminder to all. Meeting agendas should have the common goal posted at the top, and both groups should read it aloud before the meeting starts. To protect relationships, under the common goal on the agenda should be a bulleted list of group norms, or an articulated set of common expectations for the work and one another.

The norms ensure the expectations are established prior to working together so that it is not awkward when a disagreement arises and it does not have to be corrected in the moment.

NORMING THE GROUP WORK

Norms are simply agreements. Norms should include the time the group agrees to meet and whether meetings will begin and end on time. They must outline the rebuke others will have for unproductive behavior. They should outline how the group will discourage distractions of interruptions and sidebar conversations. The norms should spell out the confidentiality expectations and articulate when and how much information will be shared with anyone outside of the meeting group. Norms can also include ways the group will encourage participation. An example of a list of group norms follows:

As a group, in our work together, we agree to the following:

- We commit to being open to and respectful of each other's ideas and to listen generously without thinking of what to say next.
- We will refrain from sidebar comments.
- We will be critical of ideas and not people.
- We will present ideas rather than personal agendas.
- We will be respectful of each other's time, arriving promptly and giving our full attention to others.
- We will offer support and assistance to each other.
- We will focus on the common goal.

If any individual feels a group norm was violated, we will refer to the group norms in a clear but casual, nonconfrontational manner.

The most successful teams identify a common goal and the norms by which they will operate when working to achieve the goal. Similar to wearing the same jerseys or the same team color, a common goal and articulated group norms can unify, motivate, and focus members of the group. It can provide something for which to cheer and eventually celebrate. If agreed-upon norms are identified before the work begins, less conflict will accompany the collaboration, and relationships are less likely to be harmed when the inevitable disagreements arise.

The beginning of a meeting should start with a review of group norms and common goals. The end of the meeting should wrap back around to any areas that need to be clarified or confirmed. At the end of a meeting with a small to medium-size group, a skillful leader will offer the opportunity for each individual to contribute. It is helpful to establish a protocol of "going around the room" and allowing group members to provide concluding thoughts or clarifying questions. These protocols establish common ground and will still allow the opportunity for individual contributions or concerns.

While formal contract negotiations are cyclical and do not occur frequently for organizations, the need to build consensus happens frequently. Leaders should view consensus building through a similar lens. Building a consensus does not require everyone to be in full agreement, but everyone must be willing to live with the outcome of the final decision.

One tip to managing teams as they build consensus is to use a fist-to-five technique. With this technique, after an idea is shared, each member in the group holds up one hand. A fist means "I would really struggle to support this idea," and five fingers means "I love the idea and wholly support it." If any members hold up a fist, the group should stop and continue to discuss, beginning with the individual who is holding the fist.

In group consensus building and collaboration, the leader should also focus on creating an environment that encourages brainstorming and sparking new ideas. There is a marked difference between saying "Yes, but . . ." and "Yes, and . . ." Grammatically, the difference seems subtle. It is not. The former stops dialogue and conversation. The latter encourages the brainstorming to go deeper. When "Yes, and . . ." is followed by "What if . . ." powerful brainstorming is inspired (see table 9.1).

Regardless of the topic and how heated issues can become, it is the leader's responsibility to model respect and to remind others to be respectful when sharing their opinions. When a leader creates space where staff feel comfortable sharing their thoughts, she provides cognitive safety. Employees who are offered cognitive safe space are able to share their thoughts and ideas without worry they will be judged. They know ideas that may seem wild or silly can

Table 9.1. Statement Stems to Encourage Brainstorming

"Yes, but . . ."	*"Yes, and . . ."*	*"What if . . ."*
• Leader sends message of correction or challenge to a previous statement. • Brainstorming is interrupted and possibly obstructed.	• Leader adds something on to a previous thought. • Can provoke or encourage conversation to continue.	• Leader inspires others to add on and imagine other possibilities. • Encourages brainstorming and open dialogue.

spark other ideas that are viable and reasonable. The leader should ensure the group follows the most important agreement to be tough on issues and soft on people. They should challenge ideas and concepts but respect individuals and their perspectives.

During the brainstorming process, the leader should avoid simply and dismissively saying someone is wrong. Rather, show respect for their point of view. Do not ostracize them with a direct refusal. Ask probing questions to learn more about their perspective, or redirect with a portion of what was stated. Allow the person to save face.[1] This approach allows others in the room to see their leader probing for ideas while displaying respect for differing opinions. This is beneficial to all because often, it is an opposing viewpoint that helps find a promising solution to a problem.

LEADERSHIP TIPS

- Establishing group norms articulates expectations before issues arise.
- Sometimes the best next step is to stop in order to revisit a common goal.
- Be tough on issues but soft on people. Avoid making issues personal.

Chapter 10

Ethical Leadership

Women in leadership say they fear "Losing sight of my 'why,' the legacy I want to leave" and "Having the courage to do what is right, even when it means doing what is hard."

Ethical leaders have the courage to stand up for what's right. A discussion of ethics initially evokes thoughts of fiscal honesty and integrity or corruption and avarice. Duplicitous behavior, misappropriation of funds, or decisions made for personal gain are usually what come to mind when we hear the phrase ethical leadership. Without question, leaders must be trustworthy and honest. However, ethical leadership encompasses much more than those traits.

Selflessness and honoring others are also an inherent part of ethical leadership. Ethical leaders respect students, staff, families, and community members. They lean in to colleagues who can help them grow in acceptance, respect, and diversity of thought. They feel compelled to make a difference and serve as champions for diversity, equity, and inclusion. Ethical leaders stand up for those who may not be in a position to speak for themselves. They do what is right even when it's difficult.

CORRINNE'S LEADERSHIP STORY

Corrinne was in her first year as the superintendent of a four thousand–student school district with a $40 million operating budget. Beginning in her previous role as the assistant superintendent, Corrinne was always a champion for diversity, equity, and inclusion (DEI). She had initiated the organization's first DEI team and engaged community leaders to serve on the team and educate staff. Corrinne knew as the leader, it was her responsibility to not ignore but rather, to spotlight areas of weakness, start conversations, and be honest and forthcoming about microaggressions and the need for culturally responsive teaching and leading. She believed her purpose, or her "why," was to speak on behalf of the underserved.

When she accepted a promotion to the superintendent position, Corrinne knew the district was on the eve of significant budget hurdles. Fiscally, the organization needed to tighten its belt. The previous years were riddled with deficit budgets, and the fund balances were being depleted. Future revenue levels from the state were difficult to predict or count on, and the fiscal health of the organization was in question. The financial forecast was bleak.

The district faced very challenging decisions with few options. Budget shortfalls needed to be addressed sooner rather than later. As the leader, Corrinne held strong convictions about the order in which the work must be done: (1) The district needed to tighten its belt and reduce spending, focusing on items with little to no direct impact on classrooms and students; (2) fees for those who use the schools and programs would need to be increased; and then, and only as a last option if the first two options did not remedy the fiscal issues, (3) the district would need to appeal to taxpayers for additional funding.

The leadership team began with the first step of tightening the organization's belt and reducing spending. Corrinne worked with the teacher's union and her administrative cabinet to identify reductions with the least impact on students, to be spread across the organization so that no single department felt a significant effect. The high school teachers, who previously taught five sections or class periods, were asked to pick up a sixth section so each had one planning/preparation period (rather than two) and a duty-free lunch. This allowed the district to reduce the number of teachers on staff when staff retired and were then not replaced.

Next, Corrinne and her team eliminated library aide positions in each building. Each school had one librarian and one library aide. The positions were nice to have but were a luxury in times of financial constraint. The team worked directly with the affected aides and offered them positions as individual care aides for students with disabilities. Their job descriptions would change, but their salaries and benefits with the district would remain constant, which allowed the district to retain the loyal employees.

Additionally, Corrinne saw a need to reduce the administrative team. If all other areas were going to function in a lean manner, so would the administration. The district had several assistant principal/co-principal positions, which were, again, nice to have but not necessary per the organizational chart. Two positions were on the list to be eliminated, one at the junior high level and one at the high school level. Unfortunately, the two individuals in those positions were very good educators, and the district did not have any upcoming retirements on the administrative team.

Corrinne knew she needed to include the reduction of these two administrative positions on the list of recommendations for board action in the spring. She decided to be open and honest with the two individuals far in advance of official action. Yet the decision weighed heavily on Corrinne's mind and heart.

The Sunday before the first meeting was scheduled, Corrinne walked into her church feeling the weight of the world on her shoulders because of the impending news she was planning to deliver. She sat in a church pew behind a young family with a newborn infant. Corrinne thought about the way the news would affect the administrators' families.

Her focus turned back to the young family sitting in front of her, specifically to their newborn. She reflected thoughtfully and knew she had a choice. She could have chosen to bury her head in the sand and pretend the budget deficit was not a concern, or she could accept the trajectory of the impending exponential impact of a deficit over time. Corrinne knew the board would likely support her recommendations, so Corrinne felt a strong sense of obligation to make the right decision.

She watched the newborn and reflected on her duty to the infant, who in five short years would enter the school system as a kindergartener. Corrinne knew if she took the easy road and ignored the financial issues the district faced, by the time the infant entered school, the district would face significant reductions that would negatively affect her education. Corrinne recognized she could keep the budget reductions away from the classroom and students if she acted quickly, or she could ignore the concerns for several years and the reductions would require them to eliminate programs, increase class sizes, and perhaps close buildings.

Corrinne felt the weight of her responsibility. She had led difficult meetings in the past, but when someone was asked to leave the organization, it had been because they did something to initiate a termination. Employees had previously been asked to resign in lieu of termination for disciplinary reasons, but this was the first time she faced the challenge of informing someone they were doing an excellent job and the district could no longer afford their position. The district had teaching positions they could have accepted, but Corrinne knew both wanted to grow their professional careers in administration.

Corrinne approached the situation with empathy and integrity. She knew if the roles were reversed she would want to be offered grace and early notification. She would want plenty of notice before the decision was made public so she could grieve, cope, and apply elsewhere.

She met separately with both of the administrators to forecast the concept. Corrinne told each she predicted their positions would be eliminated the following year. She described how they had been outstanding leaders and she would be honored to help them find positions in other districts. Corrinne explained how the recommendation would not be discussed publicly until the following spring and they were the first to hear the plan.

The meetings came as a shock to both. Corrinne provided them ample time to think through their options and talk to their spouses. Each took a few days to process the information and promptly began applying for other positions, using the excellent letter of reference Corrinne prepared.

They were each able to secure new administrative positions in other districts a few months later. All of this occurred before the district publicized the news of the elimination of their positions. They were, therefore, able to control the messaging about their desires to relocate closer to extended family or seek career advancement opportunities. Rather than the staff and public being angry and resentful at the news of losing good administrators, they were pleased to see two beloved leaders advance their careers and move nearer to extended family.

As a leader, Corrinne put their needs and the needs of the district before her own. In doing so, she protected both.

LEARNING FROM CORRINNE'S LEADERSHIP STORY

Ethical leadership is treating others with respect and doing the right thing even when it's the hard or unpopular thing to do. It includes being a champion for all, no matter our differences in roles or backgrounds. Ethical leaders value and respect individuals. They prioritize inclusivity and fight for equity. They model respect for others in the way they make decisions. Corrinne modeled respect for others not only in her work with DEI but also in her approach to challenging budget reductions.

CHAMPION FOR EQUITY

Sometimes there are not two sides to an issue. Sometimes there is simply one correct side and then noise and distraction. When it comes to DEI, there is only one correct side. The rest is a distraction. In a world that seems to be bifurcated along political lines, balanced, ethical leadership is imperative. Ethical leadership includes respecting diversity and championing equity and inclusion efforts.

As a leader there is only one choice—to remove barriers to learning for all students no matter what. Every child deserves to be provided a safe and welcoming learning environment where education is the focus and differences are celebrated and welcomed. Public schools are designed to offer opportunities for achievement to all students, and each should be provided the resources, environment, and relationships with peers and staff that allow them to excel.

Learning must be accessible for all. Leaders must have the courage to advocate for the historically underserved, disrupt stereotypes, and challenge microaggressions in order to provide a safe learning environment for every child. As Dr. Martin Luther King Jr. said, "Intelligence plus character; that is the goal of true education."

The work environment must also be welcoming and supportive to staff and free from discrimination or harassment. Leaders are in a unique position to stop inappropriate behavior, challenge assumptions, and support students and staff who might otherwise be discriminated against or victimized. This requires the leader to be approachable, attentive, objective, and just.

Ethical leaders reflect on their role in advancing diversity efforts, influencing public policy, and sparking a cognitive debate or discourse. Small steps, when taken together with others, can make a difference in the ripple of history. Hess and Noguera encourage efforts to create a more diverse teaching staff but not in order to blame the rest of the educators.[1] Blame has no place in the improvement and inclusion. While making concerted efforts to increase diversity in staff, the leader must also address professional development of current staff so they may be culturally competent and inclusive.

Regardless of personal political leanings or the political views of board members, ethical leaders are those who are courageous for equity. They must be willing to listen to another's perspective, absent dramatic posturing and political influence. Ethical leaders value the perspective of another, even when differences are present. They educate themselves and others on diversity in an effort to improve every day.

Complacency is not leadership. Leadership requires courage. Ask yourself, "If not me, then who? If not now, then when? If I am not willing to advocate for public education, who will? If I am not willing to commit today, when will I be willing?" Leaders must prioritize DEI and accessibility through norms, policies, and programs. From a report of the U.S. Surgeon General, "This includes confronting structural racism, microaggressions, ableism and implicit bias."[2]

Public schools are intended to be the great equalizer, providing the opportunity and penchant for achievement to all who walk the halls of a school. Within the walls of public schools, children achieve beyond their families' highest hopes. Leaders owe it to our next generation of leaders to offer high-quality education. When it comes to offering a positive learning environment free of bias and microaggressions, it is not enough to be complacent with the status quo. We must do more. We must be the champions who challenge and disrupt bias.

HONEST, SELFLESS LEADERSHIP

Ethical leaders are also honest leaders. Throughout a successful career, there will inevitably be mistakes made, even by the strongest leaders. Transparency in leadership means being honest when a mistake is made. A leader might forget to file a required report by its deadline or neglect to communicate a key directive to a staff member. Mistakes happen. But if you mess up, fess up. Encourage staff to do the same, and model for them the honest approach to mistakes. When they make mistakes, staff should feel safe to share candidly in order to work through a solution to the error or oversight. This type of transparency models a selfless, honest approach.

Selflessness is key to ethical leadership. As leaders, there are times we take things personally, especially when we dedicate our passion, energy, and hours to the work. Passionate leaders in positions of power are often faced with those who doubt them. It is natural to become defensive in trying to prove your worth. However, leaders should be cautious about when to take credit and when to stand back and allow the spotlight to be on those we lead. A poised leader provides praise for others, rather than taking all of the credit herself.

Leaders are teachers. Similar to a student-to-teacher relationship, a leader should establish trust before offering critical feedback or areas of improvement. Creating a safe space allows the critical feedback to be accepted, rather than rejected with defensiveness. For example, the words *I* and *me* should not be included in personnel evaluations or when praise is offered to staff members. Leaders should force themselves to remove those words from praise comments or evaluations. "When I told her to use the new technique, she . . ." should instead be "After learning a new technique, she successfully applied it in the following way . . ." In the second option, the focus is on the employee, rather than the leader.

An ethical leader leads without overshadowing others. She allows those she leads to share her spotlight. Selflessness means elevating those around us and recognizing their efforts. Quietly or privately whispering criticism while publicly shouting praise allows employees to protect their dignity while learning from their mistakes. It ensures the individual will not walk away humiliated or deflated.

She develops opportunities for others to lead and excel. If someone is terrific, tell them. Period. Tell them. Stop trying to dream up things the person can do to improve so you have something to tuck into their annual performance evaluation because likely, the things you dream up or research are more like tips/suggestions than recommendations or things they need to do in order to be more effective. If an employee is doing an excellent job, find a way for them to mentor others, rather than searching for ways to improve what is already terrific. Praise them and encourage them to be a leader of their peers.

Feedback and performance evaluations should never be gotcha games. There should be no surprises in the process of performance evaluation or professional growth. Employees should never be surprised by what is contained on their personnel evaluations. Rather, a strong leader clearly defines expectations and then has many informal conversations about any concerns before they are elevated or multiplied. This provides the opportunity for the employee to grow professionally and to avoid embarrassment or defensiveness.

TREATING OTHERS WITH KINDNESS

Women in leadership positions who display kindness are often accused of being weak. One might suggest, "You're too nice" or "You need to be tougher." However, there is a great deal of strength in showing kindness, especially during challenging or heated situations of conflict. Displaying kindness and poise in those moments or with difficult people requires restraint. Restraint is necessary to not stoop to someone's low-level antics.

This is also where faith intersects with leadership skills. I've always thought how I treat someone else not only has an effect on my relationship with that person, but it also directly affects my relationship with God. It is tempting to stoop to another's level and return barbs or tear down the reputation of someone who launched a personal attack first. However, those behaviors not only drain energy and emotion, but they also break down a relationship of faith. Also, leading with hostility or anger makes it very difficult to be strategic and thoughtful.

LEADERSHIP TIPS

- Being an ethical leader means having the courage to advocate for the historically underserved, disrupt stereotypes, and challenge microaggressions in order to provide a safe learning environment for every child.
- Ethical leaders respect and value differences.
- Build your legacy in everyday interactions.

Chapter 11

Leadership Endurance

*Women in leadership say they fear "Not being able to sustain the stress
and pressure of the leadership position."*

A requisite for strength and endurance in the leadership role is a balance of
strength and courage, with a healthy dose of happiness. Happiness can feel
quite elusive in the midst of challenging decisions or pressures of the position. Contemporarily, the role of the superintendent has become stressful and
demanding, arguably more so than the previous decades, in which superintendents were primarily chief executive officers who focused on balancing budgets and establishing procedures or policies. Leaders who focus on building
their endurance can better fight career exhaustion, fatigue, and mental stress.
And happiness is key to leadership endurance.

ELIZABETH'S LEADERSHIP STORY

Elizabeth served as a school leader for over two decades. In those twenty
years, she experienced turbulence and sleepless nights from challenging decisions, including discipline hearings, budget reductions, union grievances, and
disagreements within the board of education. She persisted through each by
always keeping her focus on the outcome that was in the best interest of the
organization.

Elizabeth had enjoyed her dynamic leadership role because no day was
ever the same. Even through the tough times, she worked with her team and
relied on each of their skill sets to persist and to take on the challenges.

Recently, Elizabeth felt more stress than ever before as she found herself in
the middle of political debates in her community that landed on the footsteps
of her school district. For the first time in her career, Elizabeth woke up each
weekday morning feeling anything but eager to go to work. She dragged

herself into the office, coffee in hand, and began counting down to the year she could retire. Some days, she questioned whether she could endure until the age of retirement.

Thirsty for solutions to the pressure and the ongoing stress of the superintendency, Elizabeth found herself purchasing books, searching articles, and listening to podcasts on the topic of happiness. She didn't want to simply settle for unhappiness in her role. She had worked hard to get to this point in her career, and she had always found joy in it. Elizabeth wanted to recapture happiness in her work.

Elizabeth searched for the answers in her professional books, online resources, and podcasts. She learned about the power of positive psychology and the health benefits of joy. In her search, she began to question the things she prioritized and the way she viewed them. One particular author, Catherine Price, helped Elizabeth see how the word *fun* is overused and saturated.[1] Elizabeth related to the author's pointing out the way we attach fun as a description to activities or events that aren't actually fun. For example, Elizabeth used her phone for activities she had convinced herself were fun, such as scrolling through social media or binge-watching television series. But these activities didn't bring her joy or happiness, so how could they be considered fun?

Fun and joyful moments help us feel alive.[2] They aren't simply the pleasure or distraction of a mindless activity on a digital device. While Elizabeth could think of many ways to have fun with her family and friends, she wondered if there was a way to interject fun at work. She read that it is important to not take ourselves too seriously and to find lighthearted moments as well as to create opportunities to collaborate with others.[3] But Elizabeth worried that she was too busy to try to add in more activities to her day.

One morning, Elizabeth had a revelation about her priorities when a colleague asked how she was doing and she promptly replied, "Busy." Her initial reaction was to lament about the piles of work on her desk or the many meetings on her calendar. Her new understanding of happiness helped her see a fresh perspective on this automated response. She began to wonder if she was truly as "busy" as she told everyone or if she was merely distracted. Was it the many distractions that were leeching her energy and joy? There was no doubt that she had distractions all day long, primarily the distraction of her phone that she held in her hand no matter where she went. Not only was she distracted by constantly checking her emails and text messages; Elizabeth was also distracted by the draw of social media.

Elizabeth recognized that the way she used her phone for social media scrolling or mindless television binge-watching was her attempt to escape stress. By nature, the human brain is organized to seek survival, hence, the desire to escape or flee stress. The brain is wired to prioritize the escape over the need for emotional well-being and social emotional support. Many of the activities Elizabeth engaged in daily offered an immediate escape but did not set the stage for the type of flow psychologist Mihaly Csikszentmihalyi identifies as a key ingredient of happiness.[4] For example, scrolling through social media and binge-watching a new television series provide junk flow,[5] or a state of flow that offers an immediate distraction.

Junk flow activities offer a mindless escape from a stressful day but do not provide the opportunity to be thoughtfully reflective, stimulated, or creative.[6] After an hour of browsing social media feeds, Elizabeth found she was no further in the quest for happiness than prior to picking up her mobile device. She realized her distractions were standing in the way of her ability to be fully engaged. In fact, the time spent on a junk flow activity added stress because it stole time from more productive tasks and subsequently made her feel more rushed to complete them. In her quest for happiness, she needed to be more intentional with free time; limit junk flow activities; and purposefully plan time for engagement that engendered flow such as learning a new skill, listening to music, or reading for enjoyment.[7]

Flow, engagement, and happiness not only make for a happy life[8] but also provide individuals with resilience to bounce back from stress. As the organization's leader, Elizabeth wanted to also help her staff find happiness in their jobs. She recognized she could interject fun into her workday as long as she made it purposeful. She knew her employees would resent being asked to engage in fun activities that didn't have a purpose, and therefore, felt like a waste of time. Elizabeth asked them to join her in finding new ways to connect to and collaborate with one another while creating space for thoughtful activities and full engagement. Not ironically, in that quest, Elizabeth, too, found her joy as she worked alongside her team.

LEARNING FROM ELIZABETH'S LEADERSHIP STORY

Like Elizabeth, some of the sharpest, brightest leaders feel a sense of defeat on a daily basis. The weight of decisions made can be significant. Individuals depend on their leader to diagnose problems, create a plan to address each, and instill calm during chaos within the organization.[9] Sleepless nights and restless days have an effect on leaders' wellness and endurance in the position. It can feel like there is no capacity to add more stress or pressure.

Leaders who navigate through one crisis after another are left drained from exhaustion and from the time spent managing, as opposed to leading. When leaders are under attack from board members or the public, their ability to be creative and innovative diminishes. Their focus turns to defense and management of low-level tasks. Stress overshadows daily tasks, and happiness seeps from the work. Increased turnover rates in the superintendency are reflective of the weight of pressures, such as the political climate and the pandemic.

Happiness and fun are attained through playfulness, connection to others, and flow.[10] Building emotional stamina and a penchant for happiness begins with intentional steps. The first step is to *loosen your grip* and loosen your control. Consider what it feels like to drive along a highway through whiteout snowstorm conditions. A natural reflex is to tightly clutch the steering wheel until the forearm muscles tighten and burn. When trying to control a situation, we can tighten a grip to a point that it harms us physically. Not only does this create more stress and anxiety; it also expends energy in the tightening of muscles while creating rigidity.

Similarly, when we tighten our grip on pressure situations at work, we create a rigid response, an added stress within the body. We must learn to relax in those moments and attach thoughts to what makes us happy. Then, we are able to create a quiet moment of reflection to contemplate new ideas or tap into a playful side of ourselves that isn't possible when we are holding a tight grip.

Loosening the grip also means releasing control and allowing others in and being willing to connect to and collaborate with peers. Women work best when we are in a group of people who encourage and inspire one another. However, as a leader, the natural state is to be in front, alone. Being lonely incites anxiety and fears, especially in stressful and challenging times. Women often feel they need to power through alone and wear a mask of courage and bravery. Those who learn to rely on their colleagues, peers, and loved ones for support are never alone. And most importantly, leaders who learn to love themselves and tap into what makes them happy are able to endure.

After loosening your grip, consider where you draw your inspiration, where you find yourself in a state of flow. Are you motivated by listening to music, reading, listening to podcasts, being with people who offer new and fresh ideas? Perhaps there is a location that you find inspirational, such as a park, a museum, or a place of worship or a place that offers quiet solitude such as a coffee shop.

List each in the front of a journal that can then be used as a happiness journal. Or create a happiness board, similar to a vision board, with cutout pictures and words that serve as a reminder of your favorite things. Compile a playlist of motivational music. Collect happy notes or notes of gratitude others give you, and place them in a "feel good file." On the tough days, reread the emails, notecards, or letters you saved in your file.

We are happy when we choose to accent positive moments and view negative or challenging moments as plot twists, rather than failures or setbacks.[11] Those challenges signal a turning point or a point of revelation. Endurance in leadership requires a positive mindset not only about the work but also, our place in the leadership role as women. We are strong and capable of greatness if we choose to see it.

Happiness does not turn a blind eye to challenges and is not intended to be a state of constant. Rather, happiness comes in waves. It is acceptable and natural to feel angry or frustrated at times. The key is in knowing how to find the way back to a state of happiness in the darker and challenging times. Happiness should not be confused with toxic positivity or unfettered avoidance of negative emotions. Rather, it should be viewed as sunshine and a favorite song on an otherwise difficult day. We can invite happiness in without putting blinders on and avoiding sadness. When the sun comes out and a favorite song comes on the radio, we don't turn it off and close the blinds. We choose to soak it in and absorb it. We choose to allow it in and allow it to bring a smile.

Happiness has health benefits and boosts creativity, which in turn, provide the opportunity to remain in a state of productivity, creativity, and flow. Leaders must intentionally guard time for flow and connection. We must walk away from our cell phones, even for an hour on a weekend, to read a book or write in a gratitude journal. We should make it a habit to close the browser window to our emails so our creativity cannot be interrupted. As leaders, we cannot give what we don't first possess. We cannot help others find happiness if we are unhappy ourselves.

LEADERSHIP TIPS

- Finding happiness in leadership helps leaders endure.
- Fun = Engagement + Connection + Flow[12]
- Setbacks signal revelations or turning points, not failures.

Chapter 12

Burnout

Women in leadership say they fear "Not being able to endure the stress of the leadership position."

Stress is an inescapable part of leadership and achievement, but if not tended to, stress can lead to burnout, which then results in cynicism, disengagement, apathy, and lethargy. Burnout occurs when the fire of creativity, energy, and interest in a career position is extinguished. The joy that once ignited work is replaced with dullness and aridity. It is stress and exhaustion nearly every day and a psychological detachment from enjoyment of the position. It is a dread of each commute to work. These feelings are magnified when individuals do not feel appreciated or respected.

When an individual experiences burnout, they question whether they can endure the work. Because burnout creates feelings of detachment, it is likely coupled with a constant search for an escape to another job or a different career.

CHARLOTTE'S LEADERSHIP STORY

Charlotte called a meeting with her employee union leaders to address the struggles she had in recruiting and hiring new employees. The area was experiencing a staffing shortage, which created new challenges in recruitment. The organization had several vacancies, and on many occasions, a principal would interview a candidate and offer the position, only to be turned down after explaining the salary and benefits package. One social work candidate even explained she loved the principal and really clicked with her, loved the school, and wanted very much to leave her current district but just could not afford the pay cut she would take in moving from her current district to Charlotte's.

Charlotte explained her recruitment struggles to her district's union leaders and illustrated how the organization's vacancies resulted in overworked current staff with high caseloads of students. She came prepared for the meeting. She had analyzed the cost of offering a salary increase and had already secured support for the plan from her board members. Charlotte brought several examples and options to the meeting with the union leaders. She assumed they would welcome the suggestions and possibly add a few adjustments of their own.

When Charlotte presented the ideas and rationale to the group, she included increases for starting wages, for recruitment purposes. She also included a modest increase for current staff. She was surprised when after a significant pause, one of the leaders in the room sat with his arms crossed and stated, "Our colleagues are burned out, and it is more than money." He went on to explain the issues were not only in recruiting new staff but also in retaining current staff due to their feelings of burnout. There was an awkward silence from everyone, and the room suddenly turned cold.

Charlotte knew staff were stressed out but felt certain they would welcome additional compensation as a sign of appreciation for their hard work. She was not sure how to respond to the shift of energy in the room. One of her board members asked the union to provide more clarification. The leaders told stories of burnout among their peers, saying everyone felt overworked and many employees were taking anxiety medication or pursuing options to leave education altogether.

Initially, Charlotte felt frustrated, but she knew, as the leader, she could not dismiss the concerns. She needed to better understand them. She asked the team to provide her with more examples and help her brainstorm solutions. She wanted to brainstorm creative solutions to reengage all employees post their pandemic burnout.

The conversations that followed were helpful and started the path to healing. Staff felt they spent a great deal of time during the pandemic on tasks that drained them, such as paperwork and testing, reports, and oversight of protocols. Their energy and time were spent on ensuring adherence to health protocols, rewriting lesson plans to be offered remotely, and attempting to reengage students or families who were not active in the learning process.

Charlotte knew she needed to share her appreciation in words, in monetary increases, and in helping the organization reset. She felt a veil lifted from her eyes when she saw the disconnect between what the educators most loved about their careers and what they had been asked to do for the past two years. They were spending time on compliance tasks and reworking lessons to be shared via a computer screen. They no longer worked collaboratively with one another or students. The new normal isolated them from one another and from their students.

It was then that Charlotte also understood why she felt burned out herself. She, too, felt disconnected from her colleagues and peers. She knew it was time she reconnected to the parts of her role she most enjoyed, including working with staff and students and thinking creatively about how best to engage them.

LEARNING FROM CHARLOTTE'S LEADERSHIP STORY

Like Charlotte, leaders hesitate to share their personal feelings of burnout because there is an assumption that leaders should be tough and power through struggles. We've been sold the narrative that leaders must have impenetrable skin. Burnout is seen as a weakness, and a leader is supposed to be strong. Toughness is expected to overpower burnout, and when it does, it is seen as a badge of honor. If a leader shows vulnerability, it must mean she is not resilient enough to handle the long hours or carry the burden of others. It must mean she has a personal shortcoming and is too weak for leadership.

But this narrative isn't true. Burnout is a natural part of a successful leadership journey. There are moments when everyone experiences burnout. Leaders are human. They, too, feel moments of weakness. And leaders do not only battle burnout on a personal level; they also have to fight for employees who feel burned out. Our biggest mistake is assuming that what distinguishes a strong individual from a weak one is the level of stress they can endure before burning out, as if only we could rest and recharge, we could somehow reset burnout and reengage in our work.

When an individual succumbs to stress or burnout, it is often mistaken as an individual's issue, that they are simply not strong enough to endure. The causes of burnout are misunderstood to be internal weaknesses of employees who simply need to find the strength to endure. The individual is, therefore, encouraged to relieve stress with a small break or a short recess from the work, but those solutions to stress cannot mitigate burnout.

Addressing burnout is much more than carving out time in busy schedules for deep breathing and yoga or work–life balance and mindfulness techniques. Each of those is a priority in living a healthy life and dealing with stress. Burnout is more complicated than simply minimizing stress, and therefore, these techniques alone fall short in the battle against burnout. Dissecting burnout and its causes can help address it for leaders and those they support.

IDENTIFYING BURNOUT

Stress is defined by the World Health Organization (WHO) as strain caused by emotional, psychological, or physical strain.[1] Overall, health is affected by stress and how individuals deal with it. Stress and burnout are often used interchangeably; however, they are not synonymous. Seeing burnout as a stress level is a myopic view. Stress can cause burnout, but burnout more deeply affects engagement in work than stress does. It is much bigger than simply stress or a feeling of being stressed out.[2]

Specifically, the WHO provides the following definition: "Burn-out is a syndrome conceptualized as resulting from chronic workplace stress that has not been successfully managed. It is characterized by three dimensions: feelings of energy depletion or exhaustion; increased mental distance from one's job, or feelings of negativism or cynicism related to one's job; and reduced professional efficacy."[3]

Burnout can be a result of ongoing stress or a sense of overwhelming hopelessness, but it is often bigger than both. It is more than a feeling of being checked out of a task or daily activity. Burnout is a constant disengagement and despair over a job position or tasks. It is a cynical detachment from the organization that persists longer than a few days or a few weeks.

Burnout results when there is a detachment between the daily tasks of the position and one's interests and skills[4] or what one most loves about the position. A true state of burnout is more significant than one or two bad days or a brief phase of lackluster, fading interest. Maslach and Leiter state, "Burnout is the index of the dislocation between what people are and what they have to do."[5] Chronic imbalance between the two creates a cynical outlook, exhaustion, and detachment from the job.

In a society littered with perpetual technology inputs, high levels of expectations, and comparisons on social media, many leaders report feeling burned out. It is easy to blame the pace of today's work environment. The constant go, go, go feels much like a continuously running treadmill. There aren't enough hours in the day to complete the work.

Why do people quit their jobs? It is simple to slap a label on the issue and say they're burned out. Burnout is not a disposition. It is a temporary state of being when one feels their work is no longer appreciated, respected, or valued. Burnout occurs when there is a disconnect between the responsibilities of the job and the individual's areas of interest or strength.

During the pandemic, we were disconnected from one another and what we loved most about our jobs. Working together collaboratively, brainstorming face-to-face on projects, and inspiring one another were sacrificed for adherence to protocols that kept us separated. It is no wonder educators reported they felt burned out. Stress levels were at an all-time high. Managers were vigilantly focused on compliance to strict health protocols that were delivered with little preparation time. Creativity and collaboration were eclipsed by compliance and conflict. Everyone felt unsure, unsafe, and isolated.

Nearly 100 percent of our days were spent ensuring employees adhered to health compliance protocols, deflecting criticism for every decision made, sheltering our staff from the anger and frustration of parents, and balancing the fears of staff and the needs of students. This is the reason so many school leaders felt burned out during the pandemic.

Leaders were expected to set policies on public health matters, so we were expected to immediately become experts and determine whether students could safely be educated in schools, how far apart they needed to sit, what types of masks we needed to order for them, and how to ensure our teachers could educate students remotely for months at a time. Parents were angry and frustrated because they couldn't send their children to school. They were fear-ridden as their children struggled to read or to divide or to add fractions. They expected school leaders to make the best decisions, but no one agreed what that was.

We led through chaos. While no one expected their leader to have all of the answers, they trusted her to lead them through the storm. Leaders were disconnected from what they previously loved most about their roles. They were distanced from the staff, students, and peers.

During the pandemic, teachers also found themselves burned out. Teachers have a passion for helping students find the aha moments of learning, but those moments felt fleeting during the stress of remote learning. They enjoy seeing children smile when they learn a new skill, but the children's faces had to remain covered. Teachers enjoy collaborating with their colleagues as they plan fun lessons, but they were told not to meet for fear that they'd have to stay home due to a close contact if one contracted the disease. Energizing moments of engaged learning were overtaken by the management of protocols, online learning, and behaviors from frustrated students. Taken in small doses, stresses like these may not culminate to an overwhelming sense of burnout. However, when the change in the position feels permanent or pervasive, burnout also becomes ubiquitous.

In the post-pandemic recovery phase, individuals are left still feeling a high level of stress. Leaders then had to shift their mindset from management of strict protocols back to support and collaboration and joint leadership. Yet there were residual feelings of frustration and exhaustion that needed attention, and leaders too were mentally and emotionally fatigued from it all. They found it difficult to pick up the pieces and return to what was once considered the normal operating procedures.

In each phase of the pandemic, individuals were left to handle their feelings of burnout on their own. Burnout is often mistakenly assumed to be an individual's challenge, rather than a challenge of the organization or workplace. It is actually a shortcoming of the organization, rather than an individual's, and therefore, a responsibility of the organization to reconnect employees to their purpose and their passion for the work.[6] The organization must, therefore, find ways to address burnout.

MITIGATING BURNOUT

Recognizing burnout and containing it means realizing it is normal and that it can be mitigated. Welcoming stress and burnout as a natural part of growth feels counterintuitive but helps minimize its negative effect. Stress naturally occurs when stakes are high and there is a lot of pressure with much to learn. Neuroscience research illustrates how stress can develop new neural pathways, which then allow the brain to develop and grow. But the stress must be managed so it does not become chronic and result in burnout.

Burnout is natural, but the trouble is how we respond to it. We slap a label of resilience on it and expect one's inner strength to overcome, as if it separates the weak from the strong. Those who are not able to overcome it are expected to find techniques such as yoga or breathing to push through if they want to be viewed as resilient or strong.

Self-care and rest are contemporary solutions to stress. The buzz of gratitude journals, gratitude walks, and mindfulness help stressed adults deal with the challenges of work and home. But trying to balance work and life continues to plague so many.

The good news is there has been a heightened focus on mindfulness practices and their effect on good health. Unfortunately, burnout cannot be solved with mindfulness activities alone. The temporary benefits of a daily routine of yoga, deep breathing, and meditation are powerful. But they cannot address burnout.

Burnout can be mitigated, and it does not require quitting and starting a new career. Addressing burnout requires a combination of mindfulness as well as reconnecting with the parts of the job about which you are most passionate.[7]

If organizations really want to address the burnout epidemic, they must stop blaming individuals who are not tough enough, strong enough, or persistent enough and reflect on the organization and its efforts to reconnect individuals to their passion and strengths. Mitigating burnout requires reconnecting job responsibilities with what drives employees while supporting them and recognizing their efforts. This is where a leader can make a big difference for an employee. Encouraging employees to articulate what they love most about their job and what energizes them and then to find ways to connect them to those parts of their job responsibilities is key.

Deeper connections among colleagues also help minimize burnout because individuals feel supported and part of a team. During the COVID pandemic, professional interactions were reduced to small talk through video while distance between colleagues was intentionally increased. Staff were directed not to eat lunch with one another or gather for meetings over coffee because there was a fear they would all be exposed if one tested positive for COVID. Human interactions and connections changed. Relationships became distant. It was a microcosm for the negative effect distance has on working relationships and subsequently on burnout. To combat burnout, coworkers should be provided the opportunity to reconnect and strengthen their relationships.

In education, reengaging to what teachers love the most means helping remove barriers and refocus on time spent designing creative lessons, collaborating with colleagues on positive improvements, and celebrating one another and the students they serve. We must create healthier work environments and remove toxicity. As leaders, we must minimize barriers and reconnect our passion to the work. Barriers include compliance trainings, paperwork, replying to inflamed emails from parents, or preparation of materials for pre-planned vacation absences parents schedule during the school year. While it's not feasible to suggest leaders will be able to remove those barriers, we must find ways to reduce them.

As leaders, we must also do the same for ourselves. Leaders who lose their connection to the part of their work that most inspires them and at the same time see their staff burn out, feel hopeless. They may feel the solutions are inaccessible.

We, as women in leadership positions, are deeply invested and passionate about our work. We take the work personally, and when we, too, are removed from the tasks that most energize us, we risk burning out of the career. Our barriers include board meetings of angry parents or overly critical board members, spending the day justifying every decision, deflecting political heat from school leaders, or completing compliance paperwork for state agencies. While those tasks are necessary to the role, when too much time is spent on them, they overshadow the beauty of our profession. We have to plan to visit classrooms, engage with staff, and see the reasons we chose the leadership position.

Similarly, a leader's ability to reconnect to colleagues will also help her address her own burnout. The pandemic removed the social aspect of leadership. Employees are social beings and want to be able to discuss ideas and opinions. A healthy workplace is one in which employees feel their voices are heard.[8] To mitigate burnout, we must reconnect to one another and to the work.

As a starting place for reconnecting individuals with their passion, strengths, and colleagues, probing questions such as the following should be used as brainstorming tools:

- What do you love most about your job? Daily tasks? Projects? Interactions with colleagues?
- How do you spend your days at work? Daily tasks? Projects? Interactions with colleagues?
- Are your responses to the above questions aligned? If not, what will it take to realign or adjust?

The first step in mitigating burnout and reconnecting passion for the role is to identify the disconnect. After brainstorming on the probing questions above, find ways to reconnect what energizes you most about your role as a leader and why you are driven to lead. This is where you will find your passion again.

LEADERSHIP TIPS

- Deep breathing and meditation are healthy strategies to alleviate stress. However, they alone cannot cure burnout.
- Burnout cannot be addressed simply by taking time to rest. Addressing burnout requires realigning tasks to individuals' interests and skills.
- Burnout is not a downfall or failure of an individual. Rather, it is an organizational disconnect.

Chapter 13

Influence

Women in leadership say they fear "Losing sight of my 'why,' the legacy I want to leave."

As a leader, you must ask yourself: How are you making a difference? What do you want your legacy to be? What is your living legacy?

Educational leaders are inevitably predestined to make a difference in the lives of students through the decisions they make for the organization. They will leave a legacy when they are no longer part of the organization. They also make a difference for adults in the way they interact with staff and parents. This is their living legacy.

For the leader's legacy to be positive, she must be empathetic and inspiring. She must seek influence over authority, by being assertive but not aggressive. Much like what we often see in a first-grade teacher, she will build others up and genuinely care for those she leads. She has an influence on others that shapes the vision for the organization.

HEATHER'S LEADERSHIP STORY

Heather grew up with a dream of becoming a first-grade teacher. Her first-grade teacher was someone she always admired. Mrs. Bohn had a bright, genuine smile and made every child feel uniquely special. Heather loved learning to read because Mrs. Bohn made it a positive experience. It never felt like a struggle. She celebrated every success, no matter how small, and children responded positively.

As long as Heather can remember, she wanted to be like Mrs. Bohn. She went to college to become an elementary teacher and knew she would work very hard to make children feel as special as she did in first grade. She knew Mrs. Bohn taught students so much more than academics. With her warm smile that shone in her eyes as she knelt down next to a student, Mrs. Bohn communicated love and care for every child she met.

In one of Heather's undergraduate college courses, the professor asked the class whom they most admired. Every student wrote a reflection and then began to share with the class. Heather was surprised she was the only person who wrote a teacher's name. Her peers listed celebrities, professional athletes, and wealthy business innovators. Before it was her turn to share, Heather began to question if she would sound silly and juvenile if she explained the warmth her heart felt when Mrs. Bohn smiled at her as she walked into her first-grade classroom.

Heather frantically searched her memory for a famous past president or groundbreaking historical figure she could change her answer to before she was called upon. She felt both the pressure of the potentially embarrassing moment and the tug of emotion about her genuine answer. When the professor made it around the room to Heather, she boldly explained how her first-grade teacher was the spark of her life who made her feel like the most important little person she'd ever met.

Heather explained how she knew Mrs. Bohn had been the same for every student she ever taught. Heather remembered a time when a boy in her class told her she was not allowed to play kickball with the boys. While it seemed a simple childhood disagreement, Heather recalled how Mrs. Bohn turned the lesson into one that shaped both of their beliefs on gender bias. Mrs. Bohn didn't dismiss the statement or punish the boy. Rather, she took the time to address gender equality at a level her first-graders could understand. She thoughtfully illustrated for the children how there are no limits to what girls can do.

Mrs. Bohn instilled confidence in her young female leaders. Heather now recognized that the lesson was an important step in her journey that gave her the confidence to attend college and aspire to a profession in teaching. As Heather recalled memories of these lessons, she realized Mrs. Bohn's leadership changed lives.

Heather told her college peers that her life would be fulfilled if she could be the same for even one child. Unexpectedly, she felt a tear roll down her cheek as she recalled the memory. She was touched to look around the class after introducing them to her idol because she saw the power her story had on her peers. Her classmates did not see her answer as juvenile. They saw it as authentic and heartwarming. In that moment, Heather felt a sense of pride as she shared that story, which strengthened her dream to become an influential teacher like Mrs. Bohn.

While her peers admired political leaders, successful business leaders, and talented athletes, Heather recognized the power of Mrs. Bohn's legacy. Mrs. Bohn instilled in young children a desire to lead with genuine hearts. She used her classroom as a stage to inspire them to love one another and lead one another. Mrs. Bohn's greatest desire was to help each child reach their highest potential, who would then turn around and help lift another. Heather set out to continue this legacy through her own leadership story and her own influence on students.

LEARNING FROM HEATHER'S LEADERSHIP STORY

Teachers are leaders of the next generation. They influence the way children interact with one another on a playground so they will later interact well as adults. Playground disagreements and classroom misunderstandings are the lessons of influence teachers are privileged to guide.

Recent generations—Millennials, Gen Z, and Gen Alpha—are fascinated by the number of followers an individual has on social media platforms. Fashion and style trends are established by influencers who garner the most followers. Influencer marketing is a relatively new phenomenon, which refers to a user on social media with a large audience and implied credibility within a specific industry. Some may fabricate influence with beautiful photoshopped, airbrushed pictures, while others may connect to a celebrity to gain social status.

It is time for public educators to be the influencers and establish the trends. Public educators who go above and beyond are influencers who are marketing good character, commitment to learning, cooperation, collaboration, and innovation. These characteristics will determine future success. An airbrushed photo will not.

Influencers should be based on actions like picking up the pieces others have discarded—not just the garbage on the way into a school or business—the pieces of one another we may have previously discarded. Leaders should be hopeful influencers, as luminaries to a positive future. Our students only have one second-grade year, one third-grade year, and so on. They deserve our assurance it will be a positive experience.

Public educators are highly trained, skilled, and resourceful. Their passion for helping students reach the aha moments drives their desire to put in hours beyond the school bell and the school year. I am reminded of this on a regular basis when I hear stories from classrooms or witness them firsthand. In one classroom, a teacher kneels next to a student, looks them in the eye, gives them the courage to keep trying to solve a difficult math problem, and then offers a high-five when they do. In the classroom next door, a teacher spends her lunch break calling a parent to explain the results of a recent assessment and the interventions she will put in place to help bridge gaps in the student's skills.

Across town in another school, a principal and social worker make sure a student eats breakfast every morning and is given the opportunity to flourish academically and socially. At the same time, coaches and club sponsors give up time with their own families to spend the day at a meet, tournament, or field trip, all the while connecting to students and encouraging them to explore their interests and talents. These are the stories of public education and public educators.

Educational leaders influence others in a positive way. Women in leadership see themselves in a position to influence fellow women as well as young girls who aspire to also flip the status quo. Women can influence one another by elevating and celebrating them.

Female leaders still face stereotypes, especially in the role of the superintendent. Because we work in a male-dominated career, we battle stereotypes and misconceptions that we cannot handle issues typically viewed as areas of mastery for our male colleagues, such as finance and construction or building maintenance. We are more than capable of leading those areas, especially when we build a strong team of subject matter experts who can see to the daily needs and details. Being willing to take on roles historically identified as male-dominated not only allows us the opportunity to shine, but it shows the young girls in our classrooms how they, too, can lead at an executive level. We influence their dreams by modeling our successful achievements of our own dreams. By challenging stereotypes, we inspire and influence younger generations!

We can choose to leave a little dent in the world, or we can choose to make a splash and a ripple of infinite impact on others. It is our choice to make the legacy we leave. A leader's legacy is determined by the way she leads an organization as well as the way she leaves an organization. Her goal should not only be to generate more followers but also to cultivate and support more leaders. She should strive to amplify the voices of those she leads and to have a positive influence on them.

LEADERSHIP TIPS

- Be the example. See yourself as an influencer.
- Design opportunities for others to lead and build their capacity for leadership.
- Celebrate fellow women in leadership as selfless influencers and models of leadership.

Conclusion

Women in leadership share common fears about their roles. To overcome them, female leaders must face their fears and name them, rather than ruminating on them. Leaning on and learning from one another's stories allows leaders to see they are not alone in their fears and their fears can be conquered.

While leadership is challenging, the ability to see a positive, hopeful outlook helps leaders endure. There will always be stressors and challenges, but a glass-half-full view fosters strength and happiness. When we reconnect to the inspiration and joyous part of our work, we can successfully combat the inevitable burnout of a high-stress leadership role. The best leaders want to inspire and influence, rather than command and demand. They are instructional leaders, relationship builders, culture developers, strong communicators, problem solvers, optimistic empaths, organized, adaptive, flexible, and agile active listeners. They are you.

YOUR LEADERSHIP STORY

Everyone has a story to tell. This book narrates the stories of strong female leaders who embraced challenges and learned from them. They each became a better leader in the act of leading. They learned, grew professionally, and empowered others. They turned their fears into lessons and courageously persisted.

Your leadership story has yet to be written. Whether you are in the first years of leadership, aspiring to become a leader, or nearing retirement, your story has not been concluded. I encourage you to thoughtfully consider: What is your leadership story? What brought you to this place of leadership and what keeps you motivated to continue? Would you still be a leader without your title? Would you still want to be a leader if you had never been given a title or a pay raise? What legacy will you leave in your organization?

A legacy is not built by a special program or initiative the leader designs. It isn't established by a newly constructed facility she helped plan. It is built in the way she interacts with others daily, the way she treats individuals, and the culture she models.

Consider the goals you want to accomplish and the legacy you will leave in the way you made others feel. The joy and hope you bring to the leadership role is sparked when it lights the way for others.

LEARNING FROM OUR COLLECTION OF LEADERSHIP STORIES

Even the most confident female leaders face fears or judgments they must overpower. Each of us has experiences that rattle our confidence, but when we choose to treat them as lessons, we win. When fears creep in, we must recognize and name them, rather than ruminate on them.

A confident leader is one of empathy and competence who shares her story and elevates her peers. She embraces lessons of self-care, empathy, and competence. She takes care of herself, her organization, and her family by intentionally planning her use of time, energy, and emotions.

We must find a healthy outlet to disconnect from the inevitable stress of leadership but also find inspiration to jump back in during challenging times. This allows us to lead with poise and grace throughout the journey. Valet key-rings represent a leader's desire to be able to turn off the work and stress and focus on faith, family, and friends. The physical act of removing keys allows the stress to be compartmentalized without creating a callus outlook on the work. The people you are closest to, within your home and your heart, are those who love you. They deserve your best. They deserve to have you leave your stressors at the garage door before you enter your home. Unfastening work keys is a physical reminder to let go of work responsibilities and stress so family and close friends can have 100 percent of your attention.

Leading means quietly and privately addressing areas of concern in a manner that maintains respect while setting clear expectations for improvement. No one, in any organization, ever said, "My boss thanks me too much." Strong leaders whisper criticism and shout praise. Whispering criticism models respect for others. It allows a staff member's self-value to remain intact while the leader offers coaching and support. A system that shouts praise publicly honors and respects individual accomplishments.

Comfy shoes represent an engaged, dynamic leader who wants to get out and move around the organization. She wants to know staff members by name. She wants to celebrate their accomplishments and empathize with their challenges. She desires the time to celebrate student success and wants to be part of solutions to help overcome obstacles. Uncomfortable shoes can be a barrier to engagement. A leader may never know how much it means to a staff member when she expresses kindness and sincerity. The simple act of speaking directly to staff, asking how they are, and checking in can mean a lot.

When we elevate and celebrate one another, we grow our network circle. A circle is one we can lean into for guidance and support. But perhaps more significantly, when female leaders find ourselves on stable footing, we must reach back from within the circle to pull others in. Reaching out with selfless acts of inclusion, praise, and gratitude feeds our souls and supports our colleagues who might be quietly forging through challenges in isolation.

Your leadership story is yours to write and yours to share so that others may also find inspiration from you. Listen to the stories of other women in leadership. They will provide inspiration and guidance. Celebrate their successes, but also praise yourself for your own journey to your mountaintop achievements.

LEADERSHIP TIPS

- Network. Grow your circle.
- When you feel confident, turn around, reach back, and pull someone else into your circle with you.
- When you feel weak, lean into your circle for support.
- Be unapologetically you.
- Author YOUR leadership story—the beginning, the middle, and the mountaintop summit.

REWRITING A NEGATIVE STORY: REVISING THE QUESTION

I have a clear memory of the interview for my first superintendency. When the male board member, an elected official, said, "I want to ask her the gender question," everyone in the room knew he was expressing doubt of my ability as a woman in leadership. I felt his comment pierce my confidence because everyone in the room inferred the meaning by his tone before he even finished the question. He had never questioned my ability to lead when I was in the assistant superintendent position, the second in command. It was only when a respected female applied for the district's top position that he questioned whether gender would stand in the way of success. To make matters worse, he and the board knew I was already taking on those responsibilities because the male superintendent traveled often in his last years in the role. While he was away from the office, I assumed and completed the duties of the position. Yet now this board member doubted whether a woman could handle those duties.

I was both alarmed and offended by his question. I was the board's only female candidate and would be the district's first female superintendent. This elected official audibly questioned how I could handle the top leadership position of a multi-million dollar school district with over five hundred employees and four thousand students. He audibly doubted my potential solely because I was a female candidate for the prestigious executive leadership position. He expected me to explain how I could handle the pressures of the position as a woman.

The interview was a microcosm of a wider concern. The board member saw nothing wrong with his question. The rest of the room felt uncomfortable with the implication, but it wasn't until a female board member spoke out that the sexist comment was called out. Her leadership in that moment was strong because she recognized his bias and promptly confronted and redirected him. When he challenged her redirection, she persisted. Having a female leader in the room can help address gender bias in the organization. She can promptly address subtle or implied bias within the organization, just as the female board member did.

Through my research on women in leadership and my interactions with very strong, capable female leaders, I have found clarity in his ignorance. In retrospect, I have chosen to see his question through a different lens. I choose to reframe his point for the younger version of myself who sat in that interview room over a decade ago, frozen in awkward silence as he vocalized his gender bias.

I would whisper in her ear that she should tell him the answer to his doubt of my ability is grounded in his bias and misogynist views. I would tell the younger version of myself that she is capable and would prove her worth in the many successes to follow that experience. I would tell her she shouldn't have been asked to explain how her gender would influence her ability to lead or how she might overcome his ill-conceived judgments of her shortcomings as a female.

I would have told the younger version of myself he was wrong and that his blunder was a lesson. The gender question should not be a question of doubt and gender bias. Rather, the gender question could be far more insightful and influential. The gender question should help identify the unique and exceptional ways women lead. It should question ways to increase access for women to move from middle management to high-level leadership roles. The gender question should ask what ways we can shatter glass ceilings of pay and opportunity. It should be a question that challenges stereotypes and biases and the way they hold women back or perpetuate their fears.

Reframing the gender question offers the opportunity to explore the resources, connections, and experiences women need to exceed in their highest dreams. It inspires exploration of the ways women can support themselves and one another. The gender question should be one that sheds light on the way women can strengthen their confidence, and influence the next generation of leaders. It should explore ways to encourage women to pursue executive leadership roles while also inspiring young girls to see themselves as leaders.

Women in leadership deserve the opportunity to reframe the gender question. They are as capable, hardworking, ethical, and motivated as their male counterparts. They bring creativity, empathy, and compassion to executive leadership. When women in leadership are provided room for self-care, honesty, and confidence, they step into their own comfy shoes of leadership and prove they deserve the opportunity to shatter glass ceilings.

Notes

INTRODUCTION

1. R. Harris, *The Confidence Gap: A Guide to Overcoming Fear and Self-Doubt* (New York: Penguin Group Australia, 2011).

2. K. Kay and C. Shipman, *The Confidence Code: The Science and Art of Self-Assurance—What Women Should Know* (New York: Harper Business, 2014).

3. S. Sandberg, *Lean In: Women, Work, and the Will to Lead* (New York: Alfred A. Knopf, 2013).

4. Sandberg, *Lean In*.

5. J. Ledesma, "Conceptual Frameworks and Research Models on Resilience in Leadership," Sage Open, published August 12, 2014, https://doi.org/10.1177/2158244014545464.

6. Ledesma, "Conceptual Frameworks."

7. Ledesma, "Conceptual Frameworks."

8. G. Anderson and J. Nadel, *We: A Manifesto for Women Everywhere* (New York: Atria Paperback, 2017).

9. Judith A. Adkison, "Women in School Administration: A Review of the Research," *Review of Educational Research* 51, no. 3 (1981): 311–43.

CHAPTER 1

1. J. Collins, *Good to Great: Why Some Companies Make the Leap and Others Don't* (New York: HarperCollins, 2001).

2. Collins, *Good to Great*.

3. Dale Carnegie, *How to Win Friends & Influence People*, 100th Printing (New York: Simon & Schuster, 2023).

4. U.S. Department of Health and Human Services, "The U.S. Surgeon General's Framework for Workplace Mental Health & Well-Being," accessed July 6, 2023, https://www.hhs.gov/sites/default/files/workplace-mental-health-well-being.pdf.

5. Todd Whitaker, *Shifting the Monkey: The Art of Protecting Good People from Liars, Criers, and Other Slackers (A Book on School Leadership and Teacher Performance)* (Bloomington, IN: Solution Tree, 2014).

CHAPTER 2

1. K. Kay and C. Shipman, *The Confidence Code: The Science and Art of Self-Assurance—What Women Should Know* (New York: HarperCollins, 2014).

2. S. Helgesen and M. Goldsmith, *How Women Rise: Break the 12 Habits Holding You Back from Your Next Raise, Promotion, or Job* (New York: Hachette Book Group, 2019).

3. P. Briñol, R. E. Petty, and B. Wagner, "Body Posture Effects on Self-Evaluation: A Self-Validation Approach," *European Journal of Social Psychology* 39, no. 6 (2009): 1053–64, https://doi.org/10.1002/ejsp.607.

4. Brene Brown, *Atlas of the Heart: Mapping Meaningful Connection and the Language of Human Experience* (New York: HarperCollins, 2021).

5. Kay and Shipman, *The Confidence Code*.

6. Brown, *Atlas of the Heart*.

CHAPTER 4

1. U.S. Department of Health and Human Services, "The U.S. Surgeon General's Framework for Workplace Mental Health & Well-Being," accessed July 6, 2023, https://www.hhs.gov/sites/default/files/workplace-mental-health-well-being.pdf.

2. G. Anderson and J. Nadel, *We: A Manifesto for Women Everywhere* (New York: Atria Paperback, 2017).

3. U.S. Department of Health and Human Services, "The U.S. Surgeon General's Framework."

4. U.S. Department of Health and Human Services, "The U.S. Surgeon General's Framework."

CHAPTER 5

1. N. Eyal, *Indistractable: How to Control Your Attention and Choose Your Life* (Dallas: BenBella Books, 2019).

2. D. Kadavy, *Mind Management, Not Time Management: Productivity When Creativity Matters* (Phoenix, AZ: Kadavy, Inc., 2020).

CHAPTER 7

1. S. Helgesen and M. Goldsmith, *How Women Rise: Break the 12 Habits Holding You Back* (New York: Hachette Book Group, 2019).
2. Helgesen and Goldsmith, *How Women Rise*.

CHAPTER 8

1. L. Leali, *Leading through Chaos: Ten Strategies for School Leaders during Crises* (Lanham, MD: Rowman & Littlefield, 2022).
2. Tom Rath, *StrengthsFinder 2.0* (Washington, DC: Gallup Press, 2007).

CHAPTER 9

1. Dale Carnegie, *How to Win Friends & Influence People*, 100th printing (New York: Simon & Schuster, 2023).

CHAPTER 10

1. F. Hess and P. Noguera, *A Search for Common Ground: Conversations about the Toughest Questions in K–12 Education* (New York: Teachers College Press, 2021).
2. U.S. Department of Health and Human Services, "The U.S. Surgeon General's Framework for Workplace Mental Health & Well-Being," accessed July 6, 2023, https://www.hhs.gov/sites/default/files/workplace-mental-health-well-being.pdf.

CHAPTER 11

1. C. Price, *The Power of Fun: How to Feel Alive Again* (New York: Penguin Random House, LLC, 2021).
2. Price, *The Power of Fun*.
3. Price, *The Power of Fun*.
4. M. Csikszentmihalyi, *Flow: The Psychology of Optimal Experience* (New York: Harper Perennial Modern Classics, 2008).
5. Csikszentmihalyi, *Flow*.
6. Csikszentmihalyi, *Flow*.
7. Price, *The Power of Fun*.
8. Price, *The Power of Fun*.
9. L. Leali, *Leading through Chaos: Ten Strategies for School Leaders during Crises* (Lanham, MD: Rowman & Littlefield, 2022).

10. Price, *The Power of Fun.*

11. C. Alwill Leyba, *Like She Owns the Place: Give Yourself the Gift of Confidence and Ignite Your Inner Magic* (New York: Penguin Random House, LLC, 2018).

12. Price, *The Power of Fun.*

CHAPTER 12

1. World Health Organization, "Burn-out an 'Occupational Phenomenon': International Classification of Diseases," published May 28, 2019, https://www.who.int/news/item/28-05-2019-burn-out-an-occupational-phenomenon-international-classification-of-diseases.

2. C. Maslach and M. Leiter, *The Burnout Challenge: Managing People's Relationships with Their Jobs* (Cambridge, MA: Harvard University Press, 2022).

3. World Health Organization. "Burn-out an 'Occupational Phenomenon.'"

4. Maslach and Leiter, *The Burnout Challenge.*

5. Maslach and Leiter, *The Burnout Challenge.*

6. Maslach and Leiter, *The Burnout Challenge.*

7. Maslach and Leiter, *The Burnout Challenge.*

8. U.S. Department of Health and Human Services, "The U.S. Surgeon General's Framework for Workplace Mental Health & Well-Being," accessed July 6, 2023, https://www.hhs.gov/sites/default/files/workplace-mental-health-well-being.pdf.

Bibliography

Adkison, Judith A. "Women in School Administration: A Review of the Research." *Review of Educational Research* 51, no. 3 (1981): 311–43.

Alwill Leyba, C. *Like She Owns the Place: Give Yourself the Gift of Confidence and Ignite Your Inner Magic.* New York: Penguin Random House, LLC, 2018.

Anderson, G., and J. Nadel. *We: A Manifesto for Women Everywhere.* New York: Atria Paperback, 2017.

Briñol, P., R. E. Petty, and B. Wagner. "Body Posture Effects on Self-Evaluation: A Self-Validation Approach." *European Journal of Social Psychology* 39, no. 6 (2009): 1053–64. https://doi.org/10.1002/ejsp.607.

Brown, Brene. *Atlas of the Heart: Mapping Meaningful Connection and the Language of Human Experience.* New York: HarperCollins, 2021.

Brown, Brene. *Dare to Lead.* New York: Random House, 2018.

Carnegie, Dale. *How to Win Friends & Influence People.* 100th printing. New York: Simon & Schuster, 2023.

Collins, J. *Good to Great: Why Some Companies Make the Leap and Others Don't.* New York: Harper Business, 2001.

Csikszentmihalyi, M. *Flow: The Psychology of Optimal Experience.* New York: Harper Perennial Modern Classics, 2008.

Eyal, N. *Indistractable: How to Control Your Attention and Choose Your Life.* Dallas: BenBella Books, 2019.

Harris, R. *The Confidence Gap: A Guide to Overcoming Fear and Self-Doubt.* New York: Penguin Group Australia, 2011.

Helgesen, S., and M. Goldsmith. *How Women Rise: Break the 12 Habits Holding You Back.* New York: Hachette Book Group, 2019.

Hess, F., and P. Noguera. *A Search for Common Ground: Conversations about the Toughest Questions in K–12 Education.* New York: Teachers College Press, 2021.

Kadavy, D. *Mind Management, Not Time Management: Productivity When Creativity Matters.* Phoenix, AZ: Kadavy, Inc., 2020.

Kay, K., and C. Shipman. *The Confidence Code: The Science and Art of Self-Assurance—What Women Should Know.* New York: HarperCollins, 2014.

Leali, L. *Leading through Chaos: Ten Strategies for School Leaders during Crises.* Lanham, MD: Rowman & Littlefield, 2022.

Ledesma, J. "Conceptual Frameworks and Research Models on Resilience in Leadership." Sage Open. Published August 12, 2014. https://doi.org/10.1177 /2158244014545464.

Maslach, C., and M. Leiter. *The Burnout Challenge: Managing People's Relationships with Their Jobs.* Cambridge, MA: Harvard University Press, 2022.

Maslach, C., and M. Leiter. *The Truth About Burnout: How Organizations Cause Personal Stress and What to Do about It.* San Francisco, CA: Jossey-Bass, 1997.

Price, C. *The Power of Fun: How to Feel Alive Again.* New York: Penguin Random House, LLC, 2021.

Rath, Tom. *StrengthsFinder 2.0.* Washington, DC: Gallup Press, 2007.

Sandberg, S. *Lean In: Women, Work, and the Will to Lead.* New York: Alfred A. Knopf, 2013.

U.S. Department of Health and Human Services. "The U.S. Surgeon General's Framework for Workplace Mental Health & Well-Being." Accessed July 6, 2023. https://www.hhs.gov/sites/default/files/workplace-mental-health-well-being.pdf.

Whitaker, Todd. *Shifting the Monkey: The Art of Protecting Good People from Liars, Criers, and Other Slackers (A Book on School Leadership and Teacher Performance).* Bloomington, IN: Solution Tree, 2014.

World Health Organization. "Burn-out an 'Occupational Phenomenon': International Classification of Diseases." Published May 28, 2019. https://www.who.int/ news/item/28-05-2019-burn-out-an-occupational-phenomenon-international -classification-of-diseases.

About the Author

Dr. Carrie Hruby has been a superintendent or assistant superintendent in Illinois for over 18 years. She has 27 years of experience in public education as a teacher, state education agency consultant, technology integration director, assistant superintendent, and superintendent.

Carrie earned her bachelor's degree in Elementary Education from Millikin University in 1996. She earned her master's degree in Educational Leadership in 2003 from Eastern Illinois University, her Educational Specialist Degree from University of Illinois at Springfield, and her doctorate in 2022 from Illinois State University. She is a recipient of the Illinois State University 2020 Peppard-Goode Doctoral Grant. Her dissertation research dismantled a surveillance-focused factory model of school improvement in an effort to promote a model that is more equitable and supportive of struggling schools.

Carrie has published numerous journal articles on the topic of leadership and presented at local and state conferences on the topics of women in leadership, finance, fiscal responsibility, and legislative advocacy. Carrie is a Rotarian in the Rotary Club of O'Fallon. She serves as the Co-Chair of the Illinois Performance Evaluation Advisory Council, and co-developed Illinois' first all-female superintendent leadership cohort called IASA Elevate.